# HOW TO FIRE YOUR BOSS AND START A BUSINESS AFTER 40

BY

CHERYL A. MAULDIN

Copyright © 2017 by Cheryl A. Mauldin

Elite Women in Business
1 Willow Creek Lane, #1202
Jonesboro, AR 72404

Ordering Information:
Quantity sales. Special discounts are available on quantity purchases by corporations, associations, and others. For details, contact the publisher at the address above.
Orders by U.S. trade bookstores and wholesalers. Please contact 870-219-6504.

Printed and published in the United States of America

ISBN: 978-0-9993822-0-2

First Edition

## *Dedication*

*Dedicated to the three most beautiful women in the world, my daughters: Brittany, Lindsay and Hannah. Always believe you are enough and can accomplish anything your mind can imagine. Be bold and pursue life with all the imagination, creativity and passion you can muster. Always know how proud I am of the young women you have become. Love, Mom*

*To my accountability partner, and the mentors and coaches who have molded me into the leader and entrepreneur that I am today. I am eternally grateful you shared your talents, knowledge and wisdom with me. I hope to repay your time and energy by helping other women achieve great success in business and in life.*

*To the female entrepreneurs I have met me along the way — your inspiration, motivation and passion fuels my desire to be the best I can be and to create meaningful impact in the world.*

# Contents

# A Thank You to You!

*Dear Future Elite Woman in Business,*

*Thank you for purchasing my book! It truly means a lot to me, because one of my core values in both life and business is **impact**. And, I hope that I can share my experience on how I built a multiple six-figure business within a few years, so that you can do this, too!*

*It's my hope that I can make an impact by helping as many women as possible find the freedom to resign from their burnt-out professional career and start a business that is genuinely profitable and purposeful. If you're reading this and you're one of those women, I'd love for you to create the life you've always dreamed of living through the insights and practices you find here.*

*If you're new to me, I'm the founder and CEO of **Elite Women in Business**, the company I built just shy of my $50^{th}$ birthday, through which I offer one-on-one and group coaching services to help women over 40 learn how to take their business idea and launch a purpose-driven business.*

*After spending decades slogging it day-by-day in the corporate world, I now have the freedom to set my own schedule, choose my own clients, create limitless income, and most joyfully, give back to the causes I most believe in.*

*Best of all, I can take my family on all-expenses paid vacations multiple times a year — as I'm about to become a grandmother for the first time, I can say that spending time with my daughters and soon grandchildren are one of the most rewarding parts about being a thriving female entrepreneur.*

*Know this as you start your journey, there are no magic-bullets or trade secrets to be a successful entrepreneur. Overnight success is a myth; it rarely happens. Get-rich-quick schemes only make the person selling those rich. You will not find any of those in this book. I am committed to providing you with proven strategies that I and other successful entrepreneurs have used to build a successful and profitable business.*

*Here's to your success!*

*Cheryl Mauldin*

# How I Went from Hopeless to Half-a-Million Dollars in Revenue — In 2 Years

You might look at where I am now and think that it's been easy to get here. In many ways, it has — in other ways, I was forced into it. (Thankfully.) I'll share a little about how my journey unfolded, so you can understand how your path towards entrepreneurship can lead to great success quicker than you think, too!

Though I've technically been an entrepreneur since the age of 18, running side photography businesses while I worked in "Corporate America", I wouldn't have necessarily called myself a successful business woman, because I found myself working seven days a week, sometimes from sun-up to sunset.

And, even with a nursing and business degree that eventually led me to become the Chief Quality Officer of a company owned by a Fortune 500 Corporation, I still found myself in six figure debt as a single mother.

I spent 24 years with that organization, 15 of which were as a C-Suite Execute, but I was completely burned out, lost my passion, and felt completely trapped.

I was 49 years old.

My comfortable salary kept me trapped, because no matter what business idea floated through my mind, I had a huge fear of failing my daughters.

Five years after I become Chief Quality Officer, I realized my job wasn't right for me anymore, but I stayed on for another decade. I made sacrifices, willingly, to provide a comfortable life for my daughters and give them every advantage I could. I'm not at all resentful, because I'm a devoted parent, and know that it was the right decision to make at the time.

I simply wish I would've known long ago that I could transfer my skills into a consultancy practice that would give me so much more enjoyment – doing many of the same things I was already doing – and earn three times what I had been making before.

So, I kept on. Then, early in 2015, my company was sold and reorganized. After devoted service to my corporation, I was immediately demoted three layers deep in middle management with a huge pay cut and substantial loss of benefits.

*How was I going to live the same lifestyle now that I was making less money?*

*How could I align myself with a new mission statement for a company I didn't care about?*

*What was I going to do now that my daughters were grown?*

I spent the prior year mentoring with Darren Hardy, publisher of *Success Magazine*, both through his free daily emails and paid programs. Somewhere in my heart, I knew I wanted to become a full-time entrepreneur, to pursue the path I had started when I was 18, so I began to take small deliberate actions in that direction.

I knew I needed to leave my job. I could not *continue* to do the same thing every single day anymore, let alone spend another decade and a half of my life there. I did not want to learn how to work with a new executive and management team. Worse still, I didn't want to simply find another job doing the same thing for a different company — my passion was gone. I was burned out. I was no longer challenged.

I felt like I could not get off this treadmill.

Yet, in the past, my part-time businesses had consumed my life. I only knew how to work *for* my business, rather than *on* my business, and no matter how hard I racked my brain, I could not figure out how to replace my corporate salary.

Then, one day, I had a crazy idea. What if I took the skills, knowledge and experience from my corporate career and simply started a consulting business? After all, I was considered an expert in the field.

What if this could actually work out...?

I thought about this for two days. Journaled. Did some research. Prayed. Then on the third day, I received a mentoring email from Darren that said, *"Do it today. Do something incredible. It could be something that you have always wanted to do, but have been a bit chicken to try. Yep, don't wait another day, do it today. That is what a mentor is for, to push you to do what you know you should do, but no one has pushed you to stretch to your full capability. It's okay if you are scared - do it scared. But do it! The thing you know you should do. Just do it now. Do it today."*

*"The thing you know you should do. Just do it now. Do it today."* – those words echoed through me. I could not stop thinking about the message. I knew at that moment what I had to do.

I walked into work that morning and wrote my resignation letter.

All I had was an idea. Still, I decided it was worth pursuing and after turning in my resignation letter, I have never looked back.

Over the course of finishing my required thirty days with the organization, I did everything you'll find in this book to create the business of my dreams, craft a plan for my life that I would ultimately truly enjoy living, and create my plan to become financially free.

**If you follow the steps in this book, I believe you can do it, too.**

I was 49 years old when I got started and by some standards, I was "too old" to start anew. Some people thought I was crazy. Some people thought it was a terrible mistake. But, with my children out of the nest and a dismal corporate future ahead of me, I was motivated beyond belief to make my OWN business a success.

I was driven by my core values to create impact and provide service.

I was inspired by the mentors I followed.

I was inspired by the people I would be able to help.

I was impassioned to create my dream life, for me and my family.

Were there bumps in the road? Of course.

Was every day easy? Of course not.

An entrepreneur's journey is more like a rollercoaster than a walk in the park. There are ups, downs, twists and turns. Every successful entrepreneur goes through failure and success. We learn from failure and celebrate success.

As often happens when you begin to follow your dreams, I began to notice there were so many other women like me, trapped in careers they felt they would have to stay in until retirement. They were resentful they were passed over for promotions to people with less experience and fewer skills. They were tired of trying to compete with younger and more energetic co-workers, just to get noticed. They made the same sacrifices I had made for their families, but in their heart of hearts they knew they were meant for more.

Is this how you feel, too?

Consider this book, a workbook. From beginning to end, you should be able to craft a roadmap for your very own business idea, so that you can go from "I wonder…" to "Open for business!"

Mark it up, use the exercises. Write in the margins. (Or, if you're the kind of person who can't make yourself write in a book, no problem! There's a great workbook with all the exercises mentioned here and plenty of blank lines to fill out.)

It doesn't matter where you complete the exercises or how long it takes you to do them — the most important part is that you actually do them! This book is designed to take you where you want to go, but only if you do the work.

An article in Entrepreneur magazine estimates that only 8% of the population pursues personal development. An article in the Atlantic estimates, of those who sign up for personal development (like reading this book, enrolling in an online course, etc.), only 2% finish. Of that 2% only who finish, only a few will implement what they have learned.

The second compelling reason to not just read this book, but also take notes and complete the exercises can be found in the Forgetting Curve. Research on the forgetting curve shows that within one hour, people will have forgotten an average of 50 percent of the information. Within 24 hours, they have forgotten an average of 70 percent of new information, and within a week, forgetting claims an average of 90 percent of it.

Over the past few years, I have learned the difference between highly successful business women and women who want a successful business is that truly successful women *act*. They take massive action, even if it means facing their own fears.

That's why it's helpful to have a coach to guide you along. And, that's what I'm here for!

Now, let's build the business of your dreams!

# Chapter 1 - Start Where You Are

While we've never met in person, there are a few things that I might know about you.

You *likely:*

- *Have a successful career.*
- *Are a devoted M-O-M, and have put your own dreams on hold to raise your children.*
- *Have been in the same job for many years.*
- *Have been with your same employer for possibly a decade or more.*
- *Have a job that has become easy, and you are bored to tears.*
- *Stay in this job, even though you are burned-out, because it provides a stable income and comfortable life.*
- *Worry about your ability to keep pace as younger, talented employees come into your organization.*
- *Shudder to think about starting over in a new organization or company.*
- *Have children who have left home for college, or you're about to have an empty nest.*
- *Often wonder if you will be stuck in this soul-sucking, unfulfilling career until you retire.*
- *Have always wanted to start your own business.*
- *Often dream about owning your own business.*
- *Know you were meant for more — you were meant to do bigger things!*
- *Really want to have purpose in your life.*

- *Want to make a difference.*
- *Want true time freedom and financial freedom.*
- *Know now is the time for you — the time you can finally say YES to YOUR dream.*

If any of this sounds familiar, rest assured — I was there, too!

I was stuck in a burned-out 9-to-5 career with a comfortable life, but **not living my dream life.** I truly hated every minute of most days and despite my healthy salary, still found myself in mounting debt.

*Was this really the life I chose?* I'd often wonder. Or, more frequently, I'd worry, "*Am I stuck here forever?*"

Have you ever had this thought, too?

I made the same sacrifices you've likely made to provide the best life for my children. I had opportunities and ideas for starting a business, but whether because of fear or doubt, I let them quietly slip away — for my family. And, I did these things willingly and without regret.

Yet, now that your children are growing up and starting their own adult lives, what now?

Are you prepared to stay in your 9-to-5 for the rest of your working life? Another two to three decades?

Think about how many years are left between today and the day you can retire. When you logically will be able to retire, not the dream year you would like to retire. Are you prepared to start a new job search, hoping just a new job will fill your life with purpose?

Are you ready to continue to bust your butt to stay on the same level or rise above the energetic millennials coming into your work place who are making a name for themselves?

I know the answer is "no".

You have a secret dream — maybe one you have never told anyone.

- *The dream is to be financially independent – to not worry about paying the bills or about saving for retirement.*
- *The dream to have time freedom to pursue all the things you could never do up until this point.*
- *The dream to live a life with purpose and passion.*
- *The dream where you own a profitable business that allows all those dreams to be a reality.*
- *The dream where you walk into work tomorrow and say, "I quit!"*

Am I right — or am I right?

One morning, two and a half years ago, I walked into work and handed in my resignation letter, told my boss, "I quit!" and I started my own business.

**It was the best decision I have ever made.**

You have pictured doing this in your head. I know you have. You've wondered what that would feel like. While it was the scariest thing I had ever done, it was also the most exciting and the most liberating, because I finally felt like I was owning my life!

If I had to describe it in one world, it would be: **awesome**.

\*\*

**Opportunities Are Everywhere — Especially For You**

Thankfully, in the modern world we live in, opportunities are everywhere! Currently, there are the fewest barriers to entry we've ever seen. The cost of starting a business is the lowest it's ever been. And, the opportunities have never been better for women like us to open our own businesses!

Here's the truth: **You were put on this Earth to fulfill a greater purpose.**

If a part of you feels that going to work every day and putting in the requisite eight hours isn't fulfilling your true purpose, there's a reason for that.

Your life's mission is bigger than your job or your career. You know it, and I know it, and that's why I've written this book.

You've likely known this truth for a while... maybe you've been operating a business on the side, or have a "mompreneur" side hustle, like multi-level marketing. Yet, you also made a choice some years ago: "My children are going to come first and are going to have the best life I can give them."

I applaud that, I applaud you! I made that same choice, and I did it willingly, just like you. I feel good about the life I provided for my daughters, and you should feel good, too.

But...

You and I were told a story when we were just becoming adults. The story went like this... "It's time for you to go to college, learn skills that will help you get a good job, land said job that you will stay in for the rest of your working career, get married and have a family, and then retire when you are 65 years old."

Check, check, check – yep, I did every one of those up to the retiring part! You, too? Great, I knew I understood you.

That was the narrative teenage girls like us were told. We believed it. We bought into it. We lived that life. And, so far, so good. Our lives are comfortable and we really do not have much to complain about.

Except...

Deep inside, you really wish you had a do-over for the career part. You really wish someone had told you, "Go out and start a business that lets you create the kind of life you want to live!"

Well here I am, saying that very same thing to you: **"You really can have a do-over with your career, and you can have it at your age!"**

If you notice the millennial crowd, they did not hear the same narrative as you and me. They are starting businesses in their dorm rooms. Case in point? Mark Zuckerberg a la Facebook fame. They are negotiating working hours and working spaces to allow them to schedule work around the life they want to live. They are building mobile apps as teenagers. They are foregoing college altogether to join start-ups.

\*\*

### *Your Age Is In Your Favor!*

Here's what I've also observed happening: Women like you are exiting stage left from their professional careers at 40 years old, 50 years old, and beyond to start businesses. They are using decades of knowledge and skills from their professional careers to catapult their business success. They are using their professional networks to build businesses rapidly. They are using their expertise to build profitable businesses.

One of the most common things I hear from women over 40 is they believe they have waited too long. They believe they cannot successfully launch and build a successful business at this stage in life. Even those who are trying with a side business have this fear.

Here are some examples to show you that 40 is not too late:

- Lynda Weinman started Lynda.com at age 40. A graphics artist by trade and working as a professor, when she could not find the kind of education she wanted for herself, she started this business. She sold it to LinkedIn in 2015 for a reported $1.5 billion.
- Nina Zagat did not start the Zagat Group until age 48. A lawyer by trade, she and her husband enjoyed compiling restaurant guides in Paris. Their hobby blossomed into a full-time business, allowing her and her husband to retire from their law careers.
- Vera Wang was 40 when she pursued her own fashion line, after being a competitive skater and journalist.
- The founders of Coca-Cola, Kentucky Fried Chicken and McDonald's were all over the age of 50 when they became entrepreneurs.

These are household names. But there are case studies from women you have never heard of that are retiring from their 9-to-5 to build successful businesses.

**Your age is not a limiting factor, unless you allow it to be.**

Here is evidence that can bolster your belief in your upcoming success:

- *According to a study of over 650 participants by Harvard Business Review, the average and median age of tech founders was 39 when they first started the company.*
- *Twice as many were older than 50 than were 25.*
- *Another study by the Founder Institute found that up to age 40, businesses were more likely to succeed as their founder's age increased.*
- *Research indicates that a 55-year old and even a 65-year old have more innovation potential than a 25-year old.*
- *In 2016, there were 11.3 million female-owned businesses in the U.S., generating $1.6 Trillion in revenue, according to a study commissioned by American Express*

According to famed developmental psychologist Erik Erikson, as we grow older, hunger for meaning animates us, making us more alive. His theory explains that each healthy human passes through eight stages of development from infancy to adulthood. The seventh stage of development typically takes places between the **ages 40-64** and centers around **generativity, a period not of stagnation, but of productivity and creativity.** Individuals in this developmental stage are supremely motivated to generate value, not just for themselves, but for others, asking the question: ***What can I do to make my life really count?***

I personally resigned at 49 years old as my last daughter was about to graduate high school. "What can I do to make my life count?" was at the forefront of my mind at that time. I did not want another 'job', I wanted to dent the universe in some way, to have an impact. To create a legacy.

In the following six months, I created a six-figure business, Relentless Consulting, Inc., that exists to create impact. Within twelve months, I had earned business revenue four times my previous corporate salary. **I paid my six-figure debt off within A YEAR,** and became truly financially free.

The time to be a business owner and the age of Youpreneur is now.

Youpreneur, a term coined by Chris Ducker, means the YOU Economy.

The YOU Economy is one where you take your valuable knowledge and skills and create a satisfying, passion-filled business, through freelancing or consulting, for example. The days of climbing the corporate ladder and living in a cubicle as the desirable destination are over!

Women are opting out of the traditional 40-hour work week to join a global network of women who are taking the future into their own hands. Being a Youpreneur means cashing in on your expertise and skills.

This is exactly what I did, and so can you.

Through the power of the internet and modern technology, invaluable resources are at your fingertips 24/7. More importantly, even if you shy away from technology, you truly don't have to be afraid of tech! I can help you make it much more manageable, less overwhelming, and totally navigable.

Collaborating with experts and teams is seamless, even if you're separated by geography. Global collaborations are now commonplace, every day occurrences. Sourcing goods and supplies through internet research to find best pricing is limitless.

Accessing infinite knowledge is absolutely a reality. No matter what kind of business you want to start, you have the tools at your disposal to succeed.

I started a part-time photography business in the early 1980's. I was restricted to suppliers by geography, and finding competitive pricing was very difficult. At that time, I couldn't use technology to outsource my work to fellow experts around the globe, because it didn't yet exist. I also couldn't streamline my workflow, because the technological solutions to do so didn't yet exist.

Fast forward to 2005, when I started my second photography business. By simply typing in a few key words into a Google search brought countless pages of results for printing and production services. Pricing information was just one click away. With the power of my mouse, I could outsource work to experts, manage routine workflows with ease, and find virtual assistants to help take over administrative tasks. I could even work with a business partner who lived in another state via video conference, text, or email.

The world we live in has evolved to create the perfect opportunities for entrepreneurs.

While mom and pop shops have been overtaken by big box giants and made competition difficult, specialty boutiques are thriving. Amazon, Shopify, and Etsy have allowed purpose-based businesses to sell their goods and services in ways they can grow and thrive.

No matter what your age, we're all on an even playing field in terms of the ability to create a business.

Except, you have one huge advantage: you are decades ahead of most others in terms of experience, emotional IQ, expertise and skills!

**It's time to own your power, own your skills, and capitalize on your experience and expertise.**

It is never too late for your dreams. But, you must take charge of your life, and create your own destiny.

*If you don't design your own life plan, chances are you'll fall into someone else's plan.*

*And guess what they have planned for you? Not much. — Jim Rohn*

# Chapter 2 – Your Business Idea

*"If you have ideas, you have the main asset you need, and there isn't any limit to what you can do with your business and your life." –*
*Harvey S. Firestone*

It's clear that every successful business begins with an idea.

An idea will remain just an idea and will never become a successful business, until someone takes action. That "someone" is YOU.

If you think you have stumbled upon an idea that could possibly lead to a launch of your ideal business, you must develop that idea, do the work, and act to make it a reality. In this chapter, we'll explore how you can bring your dreams to life, by identifying your customer, clarifying the solution you offer, defining your unique benefits, and ultimately, laying a solid foundation for a business.

But, first things first: How do you know if your idea is THE idea?

Truthfully, initially you don't. All ideas are of equal, unknown value at the idea stage. Until the first steps of proving the concept and conducting research, you simply cannot know if the idea will fly.

In fact, in the beginning, give yourself permission to have ideas that totally suck. They are just ideas at this point. The book, *"Your Move: The Underdog's Guide to Building Your Business,"* by Ramit Sethi sums it up best, "Until you give yourself creative and imaginative liberty to have completely bad ideas, you are not completely free to have your best ideas." The most successful entrepreneurs of those who continually put out ideas and take action, without the fear of failure. They fail fast and pick themselves up and go on to the next idea.

With every trial they are testing and learning. Learning about what the market place wants and gathering information. Even in failure, the information and lessons are invaluable. Often leading to the next success.

The key to success for any business, any product, any service is that you offer something that people want (or need) and are willing to pay for. This is often a solution to a problem they have or perceive they have. By our very nature, entrepreneurs are all problem-solvers at our core.

Every business provides some type of solution to a problem, real or perceived, the customer has. After this chapter, you'll find exercises that encourage you to take actions to test your business idea.

**As an important reminder: Please, do the work. Otherwise, you won't receive the full value of this book!**

The trilogy of business success comes when you do something you are good at, something you are passionate about, and something your customer needs or wants (and is willing to pay for). The sweet spot is where these intersect.

I recently watched an interview featuring Shannon Waller from Strategic Coach by my friend Rachel Lebensohn of Seyopa.com, Shannon talked about the difference between a unique ability and exceptional ability. It paralleled a speech I heard from DeWitt Jones, famous National Geographic filmmaker and photographer, when he spoke about extraordinary visions.

Your unique abilities or extraordinary visions are those things you cannot help but do.

It is allowing yourself to see possibilities everywhere, instead of limitations.

When your work aligns with what you were meant to do, that fires your passion and creative energy, effortlessly.

Exceptional abilities are things you are really good at, perhaps even mastered, but you are not passionate about them. It does not breed creativity or fill you up inside. It does not ignite your passion.

Shannon referred to this as "brown-out" when talking about a 9-to-5 career. I had exceptional abilities in my corporate career. I was very good at what I did, but I was "browned-out" — no longer passionate, I lacked energy and enthusiasm every day. I was not using my unique abilities or following an extraordinary vision for my life.

**Your Extraordinary Exercise**

Extraordinary visions ignite your soul, fill you with energy and joy, and allow your life to be filled with purpose and passion. Unique abilities are your mastery level skills that align with those visions to make it reality in your life — only if you follow that extraordinary vision. These are the things you cannot help but do.

**Write down what you are an expert in, what you do well. (If you get stuck, ask a friend.)**

**What is your passion? What do you love to do?**


**What are your unique abilities? Not just the things you are good at, but the skills and knowledge that you cannot help but do, the ones that fill you with passion, that spark your creative side, and fill you up with enthusiasm and energy?**


**Write a description of your business idea(s):**


**Describe the type of products or services you want to offer:**

**Describe what you believe your customers problem to be solved or need/want is:**

**Describe how you can make this a successful business, by what you are good at, what you enjoy doing, and what you are passionate about:**

There are not any wrong answers at this point. You are exploring and brainstorming. I want you to know that there's no such thing as perfection. I believe that we continue to come back to these points throughout the life of our business and continue to refine and tweak as we know more about our customers! The point is to get your initial ideas on paper — you will refine these as you go.

I go through this exercise with every new product or service I develop, and all the successful entrepreneurs I know use this same process.

I was half way finished with my first group coaching program. The first half had been defining my business idea and services, doing customer research and outlining my customer journey. Even though I had done the work, something just felt off. I kept coming back to square one. I finally confessed to my coach who gave me complete liberty to start over if I felt I needed to do that.

It was such a relief. I went right back to square one. Right where you are right at this moment. I did the exercises, and guess what? I was so much happier with the end result. I truly felt my business vision and mission were aligned with what I was creating. I have learned there is no such thing as perfect. The best is when it is good enough to move on to the next step.

How do you know if you are on track?

Good question. There are two key elements you need to work on:

1) Who is your customer?
2) Does your product or service resonate with your customer? (a.k.a., would they pay you to provide the solution to their problem?)

## Who Is Your Person?

*"You cannot make everyone happy. You are not pizza." – Neelabh Shandilya*

Your goal is to identify who is your ideal customer to know: who are you targeting?

Your ideal customer is the person who will pay for your product or service, and become a raving fan of your business. You cannot target everyone. You cannot fulfill the needs and wants of every person on the planet. This is where attention to detail becomes important, and an investment in the homework of this chapter is worth so much.

Businesses with too large a target market struggle to get any customers. Not understanding your customer – your ideal customer – keeps you from being able to better serve your customer. This is the number one goal: **to identify who you can best serve, who you can help the most, who needs your solution the most, and who you can provide the most value to.**

The most common problem I see when I begin working with coaching clients is they have not defined their ideal customer. They have a broad definition, but not a specific avatar. I am going to walk you through this part.

When you know your ideal customer, you can ensure that all your marketing, web copy, sales conversations, product development and messaging targets this specific type of customer. Again, if you go too general, vague or generic, you are trying to be all things to all people. Which never works.

**Focus keenly on one person – your person – your ideal customer.**

This also allows you to cast aside all the people you do not want to work with, or attract. These are the people that you lose money on, waste valuable time with, that consume all your mental and emotional energy, and just make you unhappy to work with them. Honestly, these customers are not worth your time.

Sounds harsh, but trust me – all sales are not created equal. Especially when you find yourself working with people you do not like to work with.

When you identify your ideal customer, and refine all your messaging to that one person – you send a subtle message to the wrong people that you are not their person either. In other words, you get yourself on the success track for all future business endeavors.

In all my following advice for identifying your ideal customer, I will refer to this as only one person. This is called **creating a customer avatar**, whether based upon a real person or one you completely make up. Focusing on one specific avatar allows you to be very specific about who this person is and how you can help them. You need to know everything you possibly can about this person to develop products or services, write marketing messages, engage, etc.

*If you downloaded the free assessment, you will receive a free video and workbook to take your through this exercise of developing your customer avatar, which is a profile or dossier of your ideal person. You can grab that at this link:*
*http://elitewomeninbusiness.com.*

The importance of defining a customer avatar is that it helps you answer questions concerning your offer. It gives you a point of reference to answer important questions:

- *Where should you advertise to maximize exposure to your ideal customer?*
- *What types of advertisements typically effect your ideal customer?*
- *What vocabulary and tone should you use in your marketing efforts?*
- *What story should your marketing content be telling?*
- *What problems or pain points does your ideal customer have that you offer a solution?*
- *What does your customer believe in?*
- *What causes do they support?*
- *What is their biggest struggle?*
- *What are their goals?*

These questions and more can be answered by doing some research on your target audience, and crafting the story to tell them.

**You need to go deep here.**

You are crafting a person with as much information and detail as possible. This is not about statistics and demographics of a group. Statistics are valuable when getting to know your audience, but creating an individual avatar helps in all your decision-making.

When you get to the market research stage, you will ask questions of those people you believe fit the avatar. This will help you be on-point with product or service development and marketing.

Relying only on statistics can lead you to be tempted to have too broad of an audience. When you target everyone, you attract no one. Your business needs to attract your ideal customer, and repel the rest.

When I began market research for Elite Women in Business, I was too broad.

I said my ideal customers were female entrepreneurs. In 2016, there were 11.5 million women-owned businesses in the United States alone. Trying to market to 11.5 million women would be impossible.

I had to narrow my scope, and so will you. My business coach pounded in my head that I had to go as narrow as possible, and create a niche. They say **the riches are in the niches,** and this is so true.

Having multiple ideal customers will be perfectly okay once you have launched your business, and have already achieved success in one niche. In fact, most businesses will eventually have more than one ideal customer. That's fine. The problem comes when you have 20 ideal customers in the beginning. You will have a hard time focusing marketing efforts toward any one specific group.

If, at the beginning stage, you feel you have more than one ideal customer, you should ask yourself if you have saturated that target market. In your initial launch, your answer will be "no". This is a sign to narrow your focus to the one target audience.

Once you have saturated that audience and market share, you can expand your reach. Until then, your efforts will be better spent going deeper into one target market than trying to cast a wide net.

**Effort wasted means time, energy, and money wasted.**

The more you can target a well-defined audience, the greater success rate you will experience.

Work on your ideal customer avatar now. Here are some prompts to help you get started. There is a space at the end of this chapter where you can record this brain dump of information!

**Getting to Know Your Ideal Customer**

What are the demographics and traits of your ideal customer? Maybe you know someone who fits the description perfectly. Record everything you know about this person. If you do not have someone to model your avatar after, do some basic internet research.

- *Where does he or she live?*
- *What does he or she do for work?*
- *Is he or she married?*
- *Does he or she have kids?*
- *What are his or her hobbies?*
- *How much money does he or she make?*
- *Where does he or she shop?*
- *How much disposable income does he or she have?*
- *What does he or she do for fun?*

The questions you can ask yourself about your ideal person are limitless. The more research you do in your target market, the more you will learn.

The goal is to get to the point where you know the pain points, struggles, and needs of your ideal person, so you know how you can solve them with your business or product idea.

- *How is he or she trying to solve her problem now?*
- *How will your product or service solve his or her problem?*
- *Is he or she willing to pay for the solution?*
- *How much is he / she willing to pay for the solution?*
- *Where is he / she searching now for the solution?*
- *What solutions has he or she tried in the past?*
- *How is the problem impacting him / her? What websites does he / she use?*

- *What social networks is he / she active in?*

*In the free video series and workbook I mentioned in the last chapter, there is also a section dedicated to crafting the ideal customer avatar. The link to get access is http://elitewomeninbusiness.com.*


**Use the space below to develop your customer avatar. It does not have to be pretty! You can use the free course workbook to make it pretty later. Just brain dump everything you can find out about your perfect customer.**

**Testing, Testing, Is Anyone There?**

At this point, you have an idea of an offer, whether it be a product or service. You have developed the story of your ideal customer. **The next step is crucial.**

**If you skip this step, you risk investing time, money and energy into launching a business that may not succeed!**

A good business idea is only a good idea if the customer thinks it is a good idea. A great business idea is only a great idea if the customer is willing to pay you.

**It's time to test your idea in the marketplace, which is considered pre-launch and pre-development.**

You need to get in front of your target audience and determine if your customer resonates with your product or service; and more importantly, if the problem you are trying to solve is big enough that she will pay for your solution.

**The only way to know this is to do market research.**

As I began to build my healthcare consulting business, I thought I knew the pain point of my clients. Notice the key words: "I thought I knew".

As I started to do research I found out that what I thought were the top priorities and problems of my clients were not even in their top 5 list! The majority of people I interviewed had priority problems that needed to be solved before they could even think about solving the problems I wanted to solve.

Had I gone to market with my idea of the problem, it would not have resonated with my potential clients. My potential clients had a burning immediate crisis to be solved, and it needed attention TODAY, before they could think about the solution I was planning to launch.

I conducted my research through telephone calls, video interviews, and short emailed surveys. The research phase took about 30 days before I felt like I had a good pulse on my target market.

You can get through this phase quicker or slower, though ultimately, it is not a race! However, I feel those 30 days saved me countless dollars and time by learning from my ideal market exactly what they needed most.

**Market Research Method 1: Join Relevant Facebook Groups**

This can be accomplished in several ways. First, I suggest joining Facebook groups where you believe your target market participates. See what other businesses are offering. If someone has a similar product or service to you, are customers interacting?

Join Facebook groups of entrepreneurs like yourself. Most groups I have participated in are more than willing to network, collaborate and offer constructive criticism. Finding a group of entrepreneurs in your desired space can be wealth of inspiration of education.

The fun thing about Facebook groups is that you can create polls and get feedback almost instantly. You can ask questions to better understand your customer and their needs or wants. You can soft-pitch ideas and ask for feedback from other entrepreneurs and customers.

My experience in similar groups is that people are really very helpful and supportive, especially groups led by other women entrepreneurs. I have witnessed people uploading prospective logos, book covers, course outlines – you name it – and getting a lot of very constructive feedback. Try to find groups where your ideal customers are hanging out.


**Market Research Method #2: Interview Potential Customers**

Another very successful way to test market research is to interview potential customers. Remember, only go after those people who are your target market. Interviewing just anyone will give you answers and feedback, but no one will have the same opinions as your ideal person.

New entrepreneurs tend to want to interview family and close friends when conducting research. *I recommend you do NOT do this.* Your friends and family are likely not your ideal customer, and are not the best research subjects. They tend to tell you what you want to hear, or are naysayers who cannot see your vision. To get the most useful and accurate information, you need to talk to real customers about their needs, wants and expectations.

You can conduct these interviews live over coffee, via skype, or however best that fits into your life right now. Technology allows you to be free from the restrictions of only interacting with people who live in your neighborhood or city. You can get global feedback with just a little effort!

Once you have found someone to talk to, *really talk to them.*

Invite them to coffee or a virtual chat. Create a focus group. Ask them specific questions. What are your biggest struggles? What do you think is causing this? What don't you like about your current situation? How have you tried to solve this problem?

Open-ended questions are best, because it allows you to get to know your customer intimately. You will hear the words they use to describe their situation, their struggle, and these words are gold. Record these sessions so you can focus on the conversation and come back to the recording later and take notes.

Really pay attention to the words and phrases they use, and how often those words or phrases come up in the different conversations you are having. The words or phrases that come up often are the words you will use in your content, marketing, and product development. You will be using the language of your customer, which will immediately resonate with your customer. They will feel as if you are inside their head.

Other questions to ask:

- *Have you ever paid money to solve this problem?*

- *What factors do you consider when purchasing a product or service like this?*

- *What do you like or dislike about current products or services currently on the market?*

- *What areas would you suggest for improvement?*

- *How much would you pay for this product or service?*

The next step is to put all the information and data you accumulated into useful data. Look for patterns and trends. What phrases came up often? Where there any common themes?

With this data, you can identify competitors, establish benchmarks and identify target segments. Your segments are the people who fall into your targeted demographic — people who live a certain lifestyle, exhibit behavioral patterns or fall into a predetermined age group.

I recorded my interviews, so I could reference them in the future. I made a list of the words my interviewees used, because this became important when I later created copy (or verbiage) for my audience — by speaking using their actual words, it helped to build the essential know-like-trust factor with them.

After I conducted lots of interviews, I had a written list of common problems, why other solutions had not worked in the past, why solving this problem was important, and what they wish they had currently. All of this was a WEALTH of information for me as I launched both my consulting business, and my coaching practice!

I go back to those lists of phrases and words every time I need marketing copy. I am using the words of my customer, so my target market is literally reading the thoughts they're currently having. In fact, people have actually said, "I feel like you read my mind."

Nope. I just did thorough market research!

**Market Research Method #3: Research Your Competition**

Now, let's look at your competition. Competition is inherently a good thing. For the consumer, it allows choices. For the business owner, it can provide case studies for what to do and what not to do.

Your competition may be local or global, depending on the type of business you are starting. Look for the business that is specifically targeting the same customer as you, and offering products or services like you, even if you believe it does not truly solve the customer's problem.

You can research your competitors by visiting their website, reading their blog, viewing their social media pages, reading customer reviews, or visiting their store-front.

As you get to know your competitor better – here are questions to ask yourself.

**What does my competitor do well?**

**What do current customers say about my competitor's business, product or service? Look at testimonials and reviews.**

**What is the competitor not doing well? In my opinion? Based on the market research you did. Look at testimonials or customer feedback.**

**What weaknesses do you notice? In their store front or web presence? In their marketing message? With their products or services? In customer service? In pricing? Look at everything.**

**Now, critically compare you versus them. How can you be better? How are you already better? How can you be different and unique? How can you solve the customer's need in a way not being solved by the competitor? What can you offer they are not and do it better? What makes you unique?**

No small business can succeed without understanding its customers, its products and services, and the market in general. Competition is often fierce, and operating without conducting research may give your competitors an advantage over you. It is a recipe for disaster, and often an expensive one.

# Chapter 3 - Creating A Road Map to Open for Business

*"A goal without a plan is just a wish."* — *Antoine de Saint-Exupéry*

Most likely when you take a long-distance road trip or travel somewhere unfamiliar, you use a map to get to your destination. Your business also needs a map of where you want to go. Without a plan (map) you will end up somewhere, but perhaps not where you intended to go.

**This part of the book will help you create your road map to business success**.

In this section, you'll create your road map by determining your core values, creating a vision and mission statement.

These statements will become the guiding principles for your business, and the filter through which all future decisions will run through.

Let's start by determining your core values.

Core values are what you fundamentally believe. They help you determine if you are on the right path and fulfilling your business goals. Core values create an unwavering and unchanging guide for you as the business owner.

Below you will find a list of examples of core values:

| | | |
|---|---|---|
| Above and Beyond | Entrepreneurship | Persuasive |
| Acceptance | Environment | Philanthropy |
| Accessibility | Equality | Play |
| Accomplishment | Equitable | Playfulness |
| Accountability | Ethical | Pleasantness |
| Accuracy | Exceed Expectations | Poise |
| Accurate | Excellence | Polish |
| Achievement | Excitement | Popularity |
| Activity | Exciting | Positive |
| Adaptability | Exhilarating | Potency |
| Adventure | Exuberance | Potential |
| Adventurous | Experience | Power |
| Affection | Expertise | Powerful |
| Affective | Exploration | Practical |
| Aggressive | Explore | Pragmatic |
| Agility | Expressive | Precise |
| Aggressiveness | Extrovert | Precision |
| Alert | Fairness | Prepared |

| | | |
|---|---|---|
| Alertness | Faith | Preservation |
| Altruism | Faithfulness | Pride |
| Ambition | Family | Privacy |
| Amusement | Family Atmosphere | Proactive |
| Anti-Bureaucratic | Famous | Proactively |
| Anticipate | Fashion | Productivity |
| Anticipation | Fast | Profane |
| Anti-Corporate | Fearless | Professionalism |
| Appreciation | Ferocious | Profitability |
| Approachability | Fidelity | Profits |
| Approachable | Fierce | Progress |
| Assertive | Firm | Prosperity |
| Assertiveness | Fitness | Prudence |
| Attention to Detail | Flair | Punctuality |
| Attentive | Flexibility | Purity |
| Attentiveness | Flexible | Pursue |
| Availability | Fluency | Pursuit |
| Available | Focus | Quality |
| Awareness | Focus on Future | Quality of Work |

| | | |
|---|---|---|
| Balance | Foresight | Rational |
| Beauty | Formal | Real |
| Being the Best | Fortitude | Realistic |
| Belonging | Freedom | Reason |
| Best | Fresh | Recognition |
| Best People | Fresh Ideas | Recreation |
| Bold | Friendly | Refined |
| Boldness | Friendship | Reflection |
| Bravery | Frugality | Relationships |
| Brilliance | Fun | Relaxation |
| Brilliant | Generosity | Reliability |
| Calm | Genius | Reliable |
| Calmness | Giving | Resilience |
| Candor | Global | Resolute |
| Capability | Goodness | Resolution |
| Capable | Goodwill | Resolve |
| Careful | Gratitude | Resourceful |
| Carefulness | Great | Resourcefulness |
| Caring | Greatness | Respect |

| | | |
|---|---|---|
| Certainty | Growth | Respect for Others |
| Challenge | Guidance | Respect for the Individual |
| Change | Happiness | Responsibility |
| Character | Hard Work | Responsiveness |
| Charity | Harmony | Rest |
| Cheerful | Health | Restraint |
| Citizenship | Heart | Results |
| Clean | Helpful | Results-Oriented |
| Cleanliness | Heroism | Reverence |
| Clear | History | Rigor |
| Clear-Minded | Holiness | Risk |
| Clever | Honesty | Risk Taking |
| Clients | Honor | Rule of Law |
| Collaboration | Hope | Sacrifice |
| Comfort | Hopeful | Safety |
| Commitment | Hospitality | Sanitary |
| Common Sense | Humble | Satisfaction |
| Communication | Humility | Security |
| Community | Humor | Self-Awareness |

| | | |
|---|---|---|
| Compassion | Hygiene | Self-Motivation |
| Competence | Imagination | Self-Responsibility |
| Competency | Impact | Self-Control |
| Competition | Impartial | Self-Directed |
| Competitive | Impious | Selfless |
| Completion | Improvement | Self-Reliance |
| Composure | Independence | Sense of Humor |
| Comprehensive | Individuality | Sensitivity |
| Concentration | Industry | Serenity |
| Concern for Others | Informal | Serious |
| Confidence | Innovation | Service |
| Confidential | Innovative | Shared Prosperity |
| Confidentiality | Inquisitive | Sharing |
| Conformity | Insight | Shrewd |
| Connection | Insightful | Significance |
| Consciousness | Inspiration | Silence |
| Consistency | Integrity | Silliness |
| Content | Intelligence | Simplicity |
| Contentment | Intensity | Sincerity |

| | | |
|---|---|---|
| Continuity | International | Skill |
| Continuous Improvement | Intuition | Skillfulness |
| Contribution | Intuitive | Smart |
| Control | Invention | Solitude |
| Conviction | Investing | Speed |
| Cooperation | Investment | Spirit |
| Coordination | Inviting | Spirituality |
| Cordiality | Irreverence | Spontaneous |
| Correct | Irreverent | Stability |
| Courage | Joy | Standardization |
| Courtesy | Justice | Status |
| Craftiness | Kindness | Stealth |
| Craftsmanship | Knowledge | Stewardship |
| Creation | Leadership | Strength |
| Creative | Learning | Structure |
| Creativity | Legal | Succeed |
| Credibility | Level-Headed | Success |
| Cunning | Liberty | Support |
| Curiosity | Listening | Surprise |

| | | |
|---|---|---|
| Customer Focus | Lively | Sustainability |
| Customer Satisfaction | Local | Sympathy |
| Customer Service | Logic | Synergy |
| Customers | Longevity | Systemization |
| Daring | Love | Talent |
| Decency | Loyalty | Teamwork |
| Decisive | Mastery | Temperance |
| Decisiveness | Maturity | Thankful |
| Dedication | Maximizing | Thorough |
| Delight | Maximum Utilization | Thoughtful |
| Democratic | Meaning | Timeliness |
| Dependability | Meekness | Timely |
| Depth | Mellow | Tolerance |
| Determination | Members | Tough |
| Determined | Merit | Toughness |
| Development | Meritocracy | Traditional |
| Devotion | Meticulous | Training |
| Devout | Mindful | Tranquility |
| Different | Moderation | Transparency |

| | | |
|---|---|---|
| Differentiation | Modesty | Trust |
| Dignity | Motivation | Trustworthy |
| Diligence | Mystery | Truth |
| Direct | Neatness | Understanding |
| Directness | Nerve | Unflappable |
| Discipline | No Bureaucracy | Unique |
| Discovery | Obedience | Uniqueness |
| Discretion | Open | Unity |
| Diversity | Open-Minded | Universal |
| Dominance | Openness | Useful |
| Down-to-Earth | Optimism | Utility |
| Dreaming | Order | Valor |
| Drive | Organization | Value |
| Duty | Original | Value Creation |
| Eagerness | Originality | Variety |
| Ease of Use | Outrageous | Victorious |
| Economy | Partnership | Victory |
| Education | Passion | Vigor |
| Effective | Patience | Virtue |

| | | |
|---|---|---|
| Effectiveness | Patient-Centered | Vision |
| Efficiency | Patient-Focused | Vital |
| Efficient | Patients | Vitality |
| Elegance | Patient-Satisfaction | Warmth |
| Empathy | Patriotism | Watchful |
| Employees | Peace | Watchfulness |
| Empower | People | Wealth |
| Empowering | Perception | Welcoming |
| Encouragement | Perceptive | Willfulness |
| Endurance | Perfection | Winning |
| Energy | Performance | Wisdom |
| Engagement | Perseverance | Wonder |
| Enjoyment | Persistence | Worldwide |
| Entertainment | Personal Development | |
| Enthusiasm | Personal Growth | |

Invariably your business core values typically align with your personal set of values. In looking through this list, what resonates with you immediately? Which ones speak to you and what you want to create?

**Write as many as you identify with below:**

**Narrow the list to at least three, which become THE core values for your business.**

**The Vision for Your Business**

Next, let's work on the vision for your business. Your vision will provide your provision.

Your vision and mission statements will form the core of your business. Anyone who reads through your statements will know what your business does, how you help people, where you are going, and how you plan to get there. More importantly, it will tell them what you and your business stand for.

It will also be your center in addition to where you start and where you finish. You will align your values with your business, and always feel at peace with the work you are doing.

*The vision statement relates to looking ahead, outlines your business goals and where you are headed.*

The mission statement relates to doing. This is the day-to-day operations of your business.

*Your mission statement outlines the things you will do to achieve your vision statement.*

A vision statement can be one sentence or paragraphs. It provides direction and inspiration for your business. It defines your most important goals, but does not include how you will achieve those goals.

Your vision statement outlines how you help people, the value you offer, and what you plan to achieve as a business. It is written in plain language that is meaningful to you, your customers, and to any future employees.

A vision statement is like a photograph of your future business, and provides you with direction. It should be aspirational, inspirational, and motivational. It will provide life and direction to your day-to-day business life and the reason why you do what you do.

> *Disney's vision statement: To make people happy.*

> *Ikea's vision statement: To create a better everyday life for many people.*

> *Apple's vision statement: You produce high-quality, low cost, easy to use products that incorporate high technology for the individual.*

> *Facebook's vision statement: To give people the power to share and make the world more open and connected.*

> *My company's vision statement: To empower women over 40 to create profitable businesses and create the life of their dreams.*

Some entrepreneurs like to create a vision board to have a visual reference of what they are striving to achieve. I am not a crafty DIY kind of girl; my vision board is created electronically and I use it as the screen savers for my phone and computer.

You may find it helpful to collect pictures of successful businesses you admire that serve the world in a similar way to your business. Pictures can help you discover the vibe, energy, and words you might not have thought of to include in your vision statement.

***If you choose to create a vision board, please share with me on Facebook at this link: http://elitewomeninbusiness.club***

*Now, it's your turn. Write your vision statement here, don't try to make it perfect:*

Your vision statement is continually up for review. You should not change it every month. But any time you think of a way to improve your vision statement, you can update it. Your vision statement should grow with your business. If your business gets too big for your vision statement, it is time to write a new one.

## Developing Your Mission Statement

Your mission statement explains what your business must do day-to-day to make your vision statement a reality. It is in the present tense. Any time you wonder, "What should I do today" or "How should I act today?", you can turn to your mission statement for guidance.

A mission statement is a few short sentences or paragraphs outlining what your business does to achieve its vision statement.

Look at your vision statement and ask yourself, "What must I do to make this a reality?"

Mission statements should be customer-focused, so a better question is, "what must I do for my customers to make this vision a reality?"

*Disney's mission statement: The Walt Disney Company's objective is to be one of the world's leading producers and providers of entertainment and information, using its portfolio of brands to differentiate its content, services and consumer products.*

*Ikea: The IKEA vision Is to create a better everyday life for many people. We make this possible by offering a wide range of well-designed, functional home furnishing products at prices so low that as many people as possible will be able to afford them.*

*Apple: Apple designs Macs, the best personal computers in the world, along with OS X, iLife, iWork and professional software. Apple leads the digital music revolution with its iPods and iTunes online store.*

*Apple has reinvented the mobile phone with its revolutionary iPhone and App store, and has iPad which is defining the future of mobile media and computing devices. (although personally I feel this mission statement is too promotional, and definitely not very Steve Jobs-Ish)*

*Facebook: Facebook's vision is to give people the power to share and make the world more open and connected. People use Facebook to stay connected with family and friends, to discover what is going on in the world, and to share and express what matters to them. Facebook is defined by our unique culture; one that rewards impact. We encourage people to be bold and solve the problems they care most about. We work in small teams and move fast to develop new products, constantly Iterating. The phrase "this journey is 1% finished" reminds us that we've only begun to fulfill our mission to make the world more open and connected.*

*My Business Mission: Elite Women In Business was founded on the core values of Impact, Excellence, and Service, with the vision to empower women over 40 to leave their burned-out 9-to-5 to build profitable businesses and create the life they have always dreamed of. Our mission is to develop relationships that empower women to create purpose-driven businesses that are profitable and make a difference in the world. We do this by providing resources and services that produce sustainable and meaningful impact and results for the women who join us on their entrepreneurial journey. We are creating a community of inspiration, innovation and collaboration for women entrepreneurs.*

As you can see, a mission statement is not a menu of services you offer. It is not a promotional piece (despite my objection to Apple). It is the reason your business exists, the results you are striving for, the impact you want to make. A mission statement is filtered through the core values of your business and your vision for the business. It can be as long or short as it needs to be for your business.

A well-developed mission statement Is a great tool for understanding, developing and communicating your fundamental business objectives. It may answer questions like:

- *Who is your company?*
- *What do you do?*
- *What do you stand for?*
- *Why do you do what you do?*
- *What market are you serving?*
- *What benefits do you offer?*
- *What problem do you solve?*
- *What culture do you create for employees?*

As you write, keep an eye out for buzzwords or hype that everybody claims. Cut as much of that out as you can that is not unique to your business. Keep only those that are special elements, unique or not, to your business specifically, not just your industry.

Your mission statement should serve you long-term. Make sure you truly believe in what you are writing, instead of just writing a beautiful paragraph.

**Write your mission statement here:**

# Chapter 4 - Building A Solid Foundation

*"You cannot build a dream on a foundation of sand. To weather the test of storms, it must be cemented in the heart with uncompromising conviction." - — T.F. Hodge*

Just like building a house, your business needs a solid foundation to be successful and sustainable. Because most entrepreneurs are doers by nature, we often put the cart before the horse, so to speak.

If you are like most entrepreneurs, you just want to launch your business, get it out into the world, and get to it. I am going to help you work on the fundamental essentials of building a solid and strong foundation for your business.

**I want your story to be the success story I get to tell.**

I have a friend who used to remind me that a "goal without a plan is just a dream". As I think back over the last two decades of my life, I can see that I had goals, but I lacked a solid plan. For example, with my photography business, the missing piece of the plan was to make profit a priority and to fit the business into my life, rather than fitting my life into the business.

Without that foundation, I ended up working 16 to 20 hour days, almost seven days a week, sometimes months on end without a day off. Friends stopped calling to invite me out, because, they knew I would say "no" due to work. I rarely slept and when I did, it was from sheer exhaustion. I felt as if I were on a treadmill that would not stop. Though I once loved photography, it soon became something I dreaded.

How could that happen?

I didn't have a plan on how much I wanted to work, how I'd pay myself first, how my life would look outside of my business. I didn't have a plan for profit, so money was continually reinvested, which is a fancy way of saying that I never took a paycheck.

None of this was in my plan, merely because I did not have a plan to begin with!

Honestly, when I reflect upon this stage of my life, it's one of the most embarrassing parts of my past entrepreneurial career. It hurts to think about it. When I tell my story today, it's still difficult to say aloud, but I'm sharing it with you, because I don't want you to go through the same things!

The difference between my life as an entrepreneur **now** versus then is that I actually have a life I love AND I take a regular pay check from my business. I plan for profit, taxes, growth and emergencies. All of this is possible because I built a solid foundation – I went into business with a solid plan for my life, my business, profit, and growth.

Above all else, your life plan before your business plan is my wish for you.

The sections that follow will feel like work, because it is work. This is the business building stage to get you from business idea to open for business. Creating a business that meets legal requirements, that begins with a strong financial foundation, provides protection for the business owner, and looks and feels like a real business are the cornerstones for a sustainable and profitable business.

Commit now to staying with me in this section. Even through the financial part, if that is not your thing. Even through the legal mumbo jumbo if that bores you to tears. My goal is not to be your financial advisor, and not to turn you into an accountant. My goal is not to be your legal advisor, or turn you into a regulatory compliance expert.

Instead, my goal is to help you form a plan from this point forward to provide you with necessary education to understand how to operate a successful business, so you can become an entrepreneur with the highest integrity.

So, stay with me here. Deal? Great, let's begin!

## What's in A Name?

Let's start with the basics: naming your business and operating a legal business.

You may already know exactly what the name of your business will be. Honestly, this was one of the hardest parts of my journey with my coaching business. I really struggled with this. I wanted a name that encompassed my mission statement, and allowed me to have an exit strategy. For that reason, I did not want to use my name in the business name.

It was only after working with a brand strategist that Elite Women in Business came to exist. Everything I tried or thought of before just did not resonate with me or my target audience.

**Start by deciding what you want your name to communicate.**

Your name should reinforce the key elements of your business. Your work in developing a niche and a mission statement will help you pinpoint the elements you want to emphasize in your name.

You can absolutely use your name as the business name. My business could very well have been: Cheryl Mauldin Coaching. However, because of my future life plans, I purposefully want to create a real community and a network. Having my name as the business name did not align with my vision and mission.

According to naming experts, entrepreneurs should give priority to real words or combinations of words over fabricated words. People prefer words they can relate to and understand. That's why professional business namers universally condemn strings of numbers or initials as a bad choice.

Additional rules of thumb are:

- *The name needs to sound good when it's said aloud.*
- *Use a name that has meaning to it, and conveys what it stands for or the benefit it delivers.*
- *Avoid buzzwords if possible.*
- *Initials are rarely a good idea.*
- *Make sure you can trademark the name.*
- *Don't pick a name that is long or confusing.*
- *Stay away from cute puns that only you understand.*
- *Don't use the word "Inc." after your name unless your company is incorporated.*

**Another key point is to just google the business name you are thinking of.**

What comes up in your search? Hopefully no other businesses are using the name. But more importantly what kinds of websites are associated with the words in your business name. Do porn sites come up? Like really, this is a thing. Do websites that are controversial or diabolically opposed to your values come up in the search? Does your competitor come up in the search?

**Ideally, your perfect business name is one you love and your customer loves.**

Hopefully, you can land on a name that describes what your business does. The domain name is available. The Facebook page name is available. Other social media channels have the name available. And, if you are going to incorporate or become an LLC, no one else has registered or trademarked the name.

The domain names and social media pages are especially important if any part of your business will exist online. *Having multiple different names in the domain name all over social media is confusing for your customer and will make you harder to find.*

Your branding strategy will be much harder down the road if your business and websites have different names, or if your social profiles do not match your website.

Those items alone can cause you to really struggle with adopting your business name.

**If you have your business name selected already record it here:**

*Let's run it through the checklist:*

- ❏ I love this business name
- ❏ My target market loves this business name or I feel the name will resonate with my ideal customer
- ❏ The business name is clear
- ❏ The domain name in .com, .net, .org, and .club are available
- ❏ The Facebook page for this name is available
- ❏ The Instagram page for this name is available
- ❏ The Pinterest page for this name is available
- ❏ The twitter page for this name is available
- ❏ There are no other corporations using this name
- ❏ There are no other LLC's using this name

**If you could not check everything off on this list, I encourage you to re-think your business name!**

Is the business name you chose good to go? Or, do you need to go back to the drawing board? Get this right.

Trust me, I originally started with 10X Women in Business. My thinking was 10X, like creating 10X goals.

But, here is what my ideal clients actually had to say:

*"10 times" not 10X*

*10X - "like obesity?"*

*10X - "sounds too much like as seen on TV"*

*"Too gimmicky"*

*"Overplayed and overused"*

*"Personally, I hate the whole 10X thing, it just sounds so fake"*

In doing my market research, I had included the business name. I was shocked at the feedback. One woman said, "So… your business is for women who are really large and obese?" Ouch!

My goal was to attract women who were not afraid to set BIG goals and have the cajones to go after them relentlessly. Women who had dominated the corporate space and were now ready to launch a business that could grow to six or seven figures.

I was so off-base with my name — but I had no idea at first!

10X meant one thing to me and something completely different to everyone else who read the name. I share all of that to let you know it is okay if your first name does not hit the mark. It is okay if you struggle with this part. It is okay if this takes you some time to find THE business name.

**Another helpful tip: Make sure you are legally permitted to use the name you have chosen.**

If any other business has trademarked the words, the name, the phrase, you are not legally permitted to use it. In most cases, you don't need an attorney for this task, as you can perform a free search online that looks at business names registered with the Secretary of State — that will tell you if the name is available in your state. Then, take your search to the next level and conduct a no-conflict, free trademark search to see if your name is available for use in all 50 states.

And, considering you can still infringe on someone else's trademark even if they've never formally registered it with the U.S. Patent and Trademark Office, you should also do a comprehensive search into all state and local databases (look for an affordable online service to help you with this).

**After going through the checklist, getting feedback, and doing market research my business name will be:**

**Getting Legaled-Up:**

I never want any of my clients to end up with legal issues because of how they are conducting or operating business. *Please note: I am not an attorney, and am not offering you legal advice. I am going to give you some practical guidelines to follow to be legally compliant.*

You probably do need to run all your decisions regarding this section past your tax advisor, accountant and/or attorney. The decisions you make at this point are really important. I cannot stress this enough. They are essential.

**PLEASE DO NOT SKIP THESE STEPS.**

Your business structure is the legal entity of your business. It also determines how business revenue will affect your personal assets in case of legal action against your business, as well as your tax situation.

This is where your accountant, tax advisor and attorney will become useful resources for your business start-up. Every person's situation could be different. I cannot offer you advice on what will work best for you, but those professionals can.

Instead, I'll dive into what each of the different business structures means and generally how you would adopt that structure.

You and your tax and legal professionals will work out the details.

You basically have the following choices for the legal structure of your business:

- *Sole proprietorship (a single owner)*

- *Partnership (more than one owner)*

- *Limited Liability Corporation (LLC)*

- *C-Corporation (Inc.)*

- *S-Corporation (Inc.)*

The chart below explores more of how each type of entity is structured, as well as the tax and legal implications. You will then be able to consult with your financial advisor and attorney to determine which will work best for you. Each business structure has its own advantages and disadvantages, depending on your specific circumstances.

| Sole Proprietorship | General Partnership |
|---|---|
| Advantages:<br><br>• Minimum legal restrictions<br><br>• Ease of formation<br><br>• Low start-up costs<br><br>• Sole ownership of profits<br><br>• Maximum freedom in decision-making | Advantages:<br><br>• Ease of formation<br><br>• Direct rewards<br><br>• Broader management base due to greater number of owners |
| Disadvantages:<br><br>• Unlimited liability<br><br>• Less available capital<br><br>• Relative difficulty in obtaining long-term financing | Disadvantages:<br><br>• Unlimited liability of general partners<br><br>• Divided authority |

| No. of Owners Allowed: Only 1 owner | No. of Owners Allowed: At least 2; no upper limits |
|---|---|
| Taxation Issues:<br><br>• Not subject to federal income tax at entity level; tax items reported on Schedule C of owner's personal return | Taxation Issues:<br><br>• Not subject to federal income tax at entity level; tax items passed through to the partners |
| Formation<br><br>• File DBA (doing business as)<br><br>• Will need Federal Identification Number if any employees | Formation<br><br>• Partnership agreement<br><br>• May need Federal Identification Number from IRS<br><br>• Each state may have filing requirements |

| Limited Partnership | Limited Liability Corporation |
|---|---|
| Advantages:<br><br>• Ease of formation<br><br>• Direct rewards<br><br>• Broader management base due to greater number of owners | Advantages:<br><br>• Can have a single-member LLC (a disregarded entity)<br><br>• Limited disclosure of owners<br><br>• No advance IRS filings<br><br>• Ease in transfer of ownership<br><br>• Can use different classes of |

| | |
|---|---|
| | owners<br><br>• Lower filing fees |
| Disadvantages:<br><br>• Unlimited liability of general partners<br><br>• Divided authority<br><br>• Difficulty disposing of limited partnership interest | Disadvantages:<br><br>• Large numbers of owners complicate status<br><br>• Death, bankruptcy or withdrawal of owner can cause problems<br><br>• Doing business in other states may require filing individual tax returns in each state |
| No. of Owners Allowed:<br><br>• At least 1 general partner and 1 limited partner<br><br>• No upper limits | No. of Owners Allowed:<br><br>• At least 1 general partner and 1 limited partner<br><br>• No upper limits |
| Taxation Issues: Not subject to federal income tax at entity level; tax items passed through to the partners | Taxation Issues: Not subject to federal income tax at entity level; tax items passed through to the partners |
| Filing and Formation:<br><br>• Certificate of limited partnership<br><br>• May need Federal Identification Number from | Filing and Formation:<br><br>• Articles of Incorporation<br><br>• May need Federal Identification Number from IRS |

| IRS | • Each state may have required filings |
|---|---|
| • Each state may have required filings | |

| C-Corporation | S-Corporation |
|---|---|
| Advantages:<br><br>• Separate legal entity<br><br>• Limited liability for stockholders<br><br>• Unlimited life of business<br><br>• Relative ease in raising capital<br><br>• Transfer of ownership through sale of stock<br><br>• Can use different classes of stock | Advantages:<br><br>• Limited liability for shareholders<br><br>• Unlimited life of business |
| Disadvantages:<br><br>• Organizational complexity<br><br>• Expense activities limited by charter<br><br>• Extensive regulation, record-keeping requirements<br><br>• Double taxation of profits and dividends | Disadvantages:<br><br>• Restrictions on number and type of shareholders<br><br>• Limitations on classes of stock that may be issued |
| No. of Owners Allowed:<br><br>• At least 1<br><br>• No upper limits | No. of Owners Allowed:<br><br>• At least 1<br><br>• Upper limit is 75 |

| | |
|---|---|
| Taxation Issues: | Taxation Issues: |
| Subject to federal income tax at entity level and upon shareholders when receive dividends | <ul><li>Not subject to federal income tax at entity level</li><li>Tax items passed through to shareholders</li></ul> |
| Liquidation: | Liquidation: |
| Taxable to corporation and shareholders to extent distribution exceeds stock basis | Generally non-taxable at corporate level and taxable at shareholder level to extent distribution exceeds stock basis |
| Filing and Formation: | Filing and Formation: |
| <ul><li>Articles of Incorporation</li><li>Federal Identification Number from IRS</li><li>Each state has required filings</li></ul> | <ul><li>Articles of Incorporation</li><li>Federal Identification Number from IRS</li><li>Filing with IRS to classify as S-Corporation</li><li>Each state has required filings</li></ul> |

As you can see there are vast differences between the different types of business structures. Each with distinct advantages and disadvantages. The extent of each depends upon the individual and the business. What is right for one business owner, may not be right for another.

*I cannot stress enough to consult with your accountant to determine which structure will have the most advantages and the least disadvantages for you.*

I did my own research and determined my best path most likely was to form a Limited Liability Corporation.

My accountant strongly advised against this, and instead encouraged me to form an S-Corporation. There were several reasons, but the most compelling to me was I would save an estimated $15,000 per year as an S-corporation in taxes paid. That got my attention! Needless to say, my business is an S-Corporation.

Your city, county and state may have very specific requirements and filings. Every state handles business formation differently. This book cannot cover all the various requirements for each state. Here is a resource where you can obtain information specific to your state: https://www.incorporate.com/choosing_a_state.html

If you will employ anyone in your business (including yourself), there are legal requirements as well. Such as registering with your state for unemployment insurance and workman's compensation. FICA taxes to the federal government. Check with your state to find the appropriate agency you will need to register with and the application process. Some local municipalities also require payment of taxes.

Typically, this involves just paperwork to get your account set up and connected to your payroll system.

While this section may have been overwhelming, do not get discouraged. It's okay to feel overwhelmed, but it's not okay to let this step de-rail your dreams. Each step can be worked through with the help of your tax advisor and/or attorney.

Ultimately, while seemingly complex, some of the business structures I've listed are easy to set up. Even the more complex structures can be handled by either your accountant or an attorney!

If you simply cannot afford a legal consult at this point, I recommend visiting your local branch of the Small Business Administration (SBA). You can also access resources from SBA online at https://www.sba.gov/. There is an abundance of free education and information on their website, including information on business structure.

*Here's a little more crucial advice: If you are not paying yourself, you cannot afford an employee. Period. Make sure you are taking a salary that supports you and your family, before you bring employees into your business.*

Here's a short checklist of things you need to complete to be a legal business entity:

❑ Meet with accountant to discuss which business structure will best suit your business

❑ Meet with an attorney for assistance in creating bylaws and articles of Incorporation, if you choose an LLC, S-Corporation or C-Corporation

❑ Hire your attorney to serve as your registered agent, if filing C or S Corporation

❑ Apply for local licenses required

❑ Apply for county licenses required, if applicable

❑ Apply for Doing Business As (DBA) with city and / or county, if required

❑ Apply for state registrations or Incorporation, if applicable

❑ Apply for IRS classification as S-Corporation, if applicable

❑ Apply for IRS Federal Employer Identification Number, if applicable

- ❏ Apply for state sales tax certificate, if selling physical products that require sales taxation
- ❏ Complete all local and state requirements to operate a business for your specific state
- ❏ Register with your state for state withholding of Income taxes of payroll for yourself and any employees
- ❏ Register with your state for unemployment Insurance withholding of payroll
- ❏ Register with your state for required workman's compensation withholding of payroll
- ❏ Register with the state for FICA withholding of payroll
- ❏ Open an account with a payroll service to handle your payroll, or ask your accountant to offer the service

## What business structure did you choose?

The goal is to start from day one as a legal business that will not create undue tax and legal liability to you personally, to the extent possible. Above all, you will know you are operating with integrity.

And, that's a good feeling.

## Getting Your Money Right

This section could go two ways. Getting how you think about money right. Or, keeping your business finances right.

Here is my take on money mindset. If you are struggling in your personal life with money or finances, you will struggle in your business with money and finances.

Just because you start a business will not make you a money guru. It also will not cure any limiting beliefs you hold about money, or cure any poor habits you have where money is concerned.

Harsh, but true. I promised to give it to you straight, so stay with me on this point.

**Your number one personal and business goal should be to be financially free.** Which means that you personally owe no one for anything.

The only exception is an asset for which someone else pays for, like rental property, that generates income.

My goal is to help you create the life of your dreams, which I know does not mean you're struggling to pay your bills, are one missed payment away from foreclosure, or are not saving for your retirement.

Your dream life is meant to be one where you are debt-free and able to enjoy your life, whether that means traveling, or buying a vacation home, or living abroad part of the year — however you define it, having an abundance of resources can indeed lead to real freedom.

If you are not currently debt-free, make that your number one top personal priority! Get advice from a financial advisor or credit counselor (a reputable one) to come up with a plan to make this happen, as quickly as possible.

I accomplished becoming debt free in less than one year of being a full-time entrepreneur. I felt like doing the happy dance down the street when I made that last payment. The peace of mind that comes with debt freedom is indescribable.

I am a huge fan of Dave Ramsey, and I used his principles to become debt-free and take charge of my money. I recommend his system to you as well.

But, first let's work on your mindset about money.

I am not a mindset expert or life coach, so I have just a few recommendations. If you feel you really need to work on this area of your life, please find an expert that can help you.

There are free resources, such as blogs, websites and podcasts to help you. I am a fan of Tonya Rineer of the Profit Party Podcast. Check her out! Also, Harv T. Eker has some great audiobooks on money mindset.

The most common money mindset issue is scarcity, such as the false belief, "There is never enough money and there will never be enough money." Such thoughts mean that even when you have more money than you need, you will self-sabotage by over-spending, bringing you back to the point of not having enough money.

This usually comes from your family and your childhood. Were you ever told, "Money does not grow on trees," or did your family struggle with money? These experiences make an impression on you that forms your mindset about money, even if you were not aware of it at the time.

Here's another limiting belief: "People with money are somehow bad, greedy, slothful." Ever hear the term, "filthy rich" or "rich pig"? If you ever heard these phrases from family, perhaps you are self-sabotaging to avoid becoming the pig.

Another huge setback with women is seeing other successful entrepreneurs with a similar business and believing the market is tapped out. This is a scarcity mindset as well. Competition serves a valuable purpose in business. Just because you will have a competitor does not mean you cannot create a profitable and successful business. There is expendable money in our society, which means there is enough money in the economy to support your business – if you serve a need with your customer base.

A very big limiting belief I see a lot of women have is that to serve others, you cannot make lots of money. That being wealthy somehow feels wrong or against your values. That sales or charging what you are worth feels slimy. In these cases, women end up not charging what they are worth, or really struggle with the sales process. It becomes hard to ask the customer to pay, or they feel uncomfortable stating the price.

**What limiting beliefs or difficulties with money do you have?**

**What do you remember hearing from your family as you grew up about money?**

Here's my take on money: **There is enough money in the world for anyone to become wealthy.**

- *Money does not grow on trees, but it is the fruit of your labor.*
- *Making money does not make you a bad person, it makes you resourceful.*
- *It also allows you to give and serve more people and causes.*
- *Charging less than what you are worth is a disservice to you, your family and your future. It also could hamper your success.*
- *If you are too cheap the customer may equate that to not good or valuable.*

To make the difference you want to make in the world, to make the difference you want to make for yourself and your family, your business must be financially solvent and profitable.

**Here's another big piece of money insight I believe in: Bootstrap your business start-up.**

Lean start-ups do not borrow money unless it is unavoidable.

A lot of entrepreneurs borrow money or put expenses on credit cards (big mistake) to get the business off the ground, and usually are paying for assets and expenses that are unnecessary to get the business launched.

A lot of my personal debt was created by building my photography business on my credit cards. In some cases, I needed to purchase supplies or equipment. In other cases, I did not have a plan to set aside money for equipment, therefore I needed to pay on credit. Ultimately, some of the expensive purchases I made were just not as necessary as I thought at the time. I had tens of thousands of dollars in credit card debt by the end of 2014. These days, I chalk this business up to learning lessons of mistakes I won't make again!

I started my consulting business in 2015 with less than $1000. Most of that money was spent on appointments with my accountant and attorney, and filing for the various licenses, legal filings, and insurance my business needed.

I did not hire a copywriter. I did not order business cards. I did not hire a web developer to design a beautiful website. I did not print glossy, colorful brochures. I did not buy equipment. I did not rent office space. I did not spend money on anything that was unnecessary to get my idea open for business in the beginning.

In my first year in business, I had generated multiple six-figure income, became debt-free, and had a sustainable, profitable business.

I also had a business with a profit margin of 80%, which meant I was spending less than 20% of my business income on business expenses. I did this by making smart money decisions and committing to a lean start-up.

In 2016, when I started Elite Women in Business, I also took a "lean mentality". As the business matures and makes more money, I invest from business profits for business growth. I have now hired a branding strategist, a business coach, ad strategist and a copywriter. But, I can afford to pay in cash for all of these services – because I had a financial plan.

The key is that I can pay for those services from cash inside my business, not with credit cards or loans. I want this for you as well.

Please look carefully at every single business expense and determine if it is necessary, at this stage. If not, do not spend the money.

One of my first mentors tells a story of investing several million dollars to start a business, that ultimately failed and he lost his investment. He says in today's economy he could start the same business for $5,000 or $10,000. The days of having to invest hundreds of thousands or millions of dollars to start a small business are over.

Start from where you are with what you have!

**I cover business finances in depth in the eCourse,** Elite Business Building Foundations**.** This book is too short to go in depth with business accounting. I personally follow a structured system of accounting for future tax liabilities, profit, and keeping expenses to a minimum. I teach these principles in the ELITE Business Building Foundations eCourse and if you want to learn more, visit this link. https://elite-courses.thinkific.com/courses/elite-foundations

**Business Financial Rules for Success**

Action Step #1: From your very first day as an entrepreneur, **never ever mix your personal and business finances.** Like, ever.

This requires a separate bank account for your business. If you have a DBA (doing business as), a partnership or any of the other legal business structures, you will have the necessary paperwork for the bank to open the account.

You can loan money to your business to seed your business account. But, you cannot pay for personal expenses from the business account. This creates a taxable situation. It also makes it very difficult to keep your business finances straight.

In the full eCourse, I recommend other business bank accounts to fund emergencies, growth and profit, but without being able to provide all the details and understanding, create one business bank account that should be a checking account with no fees, preferably.

**Managing Finances**

Talking about money is sometimes where I lose people. You might want to check out. You might want to avoid talking about money. You might feel intimidated, or embarrassed. You might feel as if you cannot handle the financial discussions.

It is okay to feel intimidated about money! I'm living proof it is okay to be embarrassed about your financial situation. When I arrived at the end of my Corporate America career with three daughters raised, I looked at my financial situation and wanted to crawl under a rock.

I cannot tell you how many nights I could not sleep just trying to figure out how I would ever pay off my nearly $300,000 debt. My waking hours were focused solely on how to get from one paycheck to the next.

Being a single mom, that money covered a lot of vacations, prom dresses, summer camps, dance tuition, softball gear, cheer camps, school trips, etc. I financed our lifestyle AND my photography business on credit cards. Year after year, I arrived at a whopping huge amount of personal debt.

I felt all the emotions I mentioned above: sad, embarrassed, intimidated… and planning for retirement… well, I could not even begin to imagine how I would broach that subject.

I am here to say that **you can own your money story**. You can also write a completely different ending to your financial worth.

The first step is to make a commitment that no matter how uncomfortable it becomes, you will focus on your business and personal finances. Once I decided to eliminate my debt and built a plan to do just that, I felt empowered.

I knew as I was starting a new business, I needed a solid financial plan, both for myself and the business.

The two things I focused on were:

1) Completely eliminating all my personal debt.
2) Creating a profitable business, without accumulating business debt and with a priority on profit.

This is what I want for you. No matter what your financial situation or your comfort level with finances and money, this section is one of the pillars of building a solid business foundation.

I will give you tips to empower you to handle the financial aspect of owning a business.

There are very few scenarios where the business owner should also be the business accountant. Honestly, my personal recommendation is not to be the business' bookkeeper either.

Unless you are experienced with bookkeeping, you can make mistakes that can be costly to your business when tax time rolls around. Use your tax preparer or accountant if you can afford the service. I recommend this expense be included in your budget.

Another option is to hire a virtual assistant experienced in bookkeeping. There are free and low-cost online bookkeeping services that receive an automatic feed from your bank that the bookkeeper can categorize for you.

One service I used in the beginning was Wave Accounting. I now use Quickbooks Online. At the time of writing this book, Wave is a free service & Quickbooks is $30 per month. Both connect to your business bank account and allow you to run financial reports from within the software that can be provided to your accountant. But, please heed my recommendation to allow an experienced bookkeeper to categorize your transactions.

The software can generate reports and ledgers you can provide to your accountant. In the beginning, you may only need to meet with your accountant annually to have taxes prepared.

As your business generates more money, I would recommend providing these documents to your accountant on a quarterly basis, so your accountant can review the documents and provide you with an income statement, cash flow statement and balance sheet. These reports help gauge the current state, profitability and viability of your business.

My accountant is a vital business partner. When you find the right accountant, you build a relationship that is focused on your business surviving for the long-term, and planning for your own financial future. My accountant does not charge for phone calls, emails or the occasional office drop-in. He encourages questions. If you can find a similar service, this is a huge point in your favor.

Now, let's cover just a few accounting terms and reports that, as a business owner, you need to understand.

Here are more key terms for you to know:

- An **income statement** is a financial statement that reports a company's financial performance over a specific accounting period.

- Financial performance is assessed by giving a summary of how the business incurs its revenues and expenses through both operating and non-operating activities. It also shows the net profit or loss incurred over a specific accounting period. Unlike the balance sheet, which covers one moment in time, the income statement provides performance information over time. It begins with sales and works down to net income.

- A **balance sheet** is a financial statement that summarizes a company's assets, liabilities and shareholders' equity at a specific point in time. These three balance sheet segments give investors an idea as to what the company owns and owes, as well as the amount invested by shareholders. The balance sheets takes its name from the fact that the two sides of the equation above – assets on the one side and liabilities plus shareholders' equity on the other – must balance out.

- Complementing the balance sheet and income statement, **the cash flow statement** (CFS) is a mandatory part of a company's financial reports since 1987. The cash flow statement records the amount of cash and cash equivalents entering and leaving a company. The CFS allows investors to understand how a company's operations are running, where its money is coming from, and how it is being spent.

In the first review of these documents by your tax preparer / accountant, schedule a meeting in which that person can go over these documents, teach you how to read and interpret them, and answer any questions you have.

**These financial documents tell the profit / loss story of your business. Even if you are not an accountant, you absolutely must know how to read these documents.**

By meeting with your accountant quarterly, he or she can help you estimate quarterly taxes, that are paid quarterly, saving you needless panic at year-end (and the temptation to spend this money throughout the year, shorting yourself at tax time).

### Do You Need Insurance?

Insurance allows you to protect your business and your personal assets, which is incredibly important. Determine the type of coverage you need. A reliable insurance agent should be able to tell you what your state minimum requirements are, as well as optional coverage.

You may need just one policy, you may need several. This is determined by multiple factors, including if you have a brick-and-mortar space customers will visit, if you manufacture or produce products, or if you visit people in their home. There are many business situations that could create a liability to you which could end your business, unless you have the necessary insurance protections.

Do you handle confidential or sensitive electronic data for your clients? Do you operate equipment that could harm a client or customer (such as with photographers)? Do you travel and need coverage for business laptops or equipment? Do you manufacture a product that a customer could claim caused an injury or damage? Do you provide counseling or consulting services?

This may be a significant part of your start-up, but take this seriously and cover your business for unforeseen circumstances.

If you are leaving your full-time job and have no other insurance coverage for health, life, dental and vision, except through your current employer, you will need to arrange for policies to cover these as well.

Even if you never purchased a disability policy through your employer, once you become a full-time business owner, I highly recommend both long-term and short-term insurance. This protects you and provides some income if you became ill and unable to work for a significant period.

**Your business is real. You must operate the business like it is real.**

### Time to Take Payment

The last financial piece is to determine how you will be paid by customers and clients, which ultimately, is super exciting!

If needed, consider:

- Setting up your invoice templates.
- Developing contracts.
  - These are all relatively simple to do. You can find templates for business invoices, receipts, contracts and agreements online. Try to find documents for your specific type of business.
- Determine how the customer will pay you. In the beginning, you may opt to utilize Square, Stripe or PayPal to collect payments, in addition to personal checks.
  - This will allow you to accept credit and debit card payments, at a reasonable rate. The preference for you will be made based on if you have a brick-and-mortar business or online business.

- Businesses that do not accept credit or debit card payments leave money on the table. We are quickly becoming a cash-less society.
- In the early days of your business, you most likely do not need a credit card processing system beyond paypal, square or stripe. Credit card processing services can get very expensive. Remember, only take on additional expenses when they become necessary.

If you're accepting mobile payments through a website for your business: make sure your website is fully compliant with encryption and all requirements of the government. If you have a website that accepts payments, you must have a terms of service policy accessible on the website customers can view, as well as a privacy policy. Your website must meet all the current requirements of law to accept financial and personal information. Your hosting service most likely can provide these requirements, although not at the base rate, which will incur additional fees. For these essentials, utilize services like fiverr, blogs, and other free resources, if you can find them and always be sure they're reputable.

## The B word.

The B-word here is "Budget. You knew this was coming. From the beginning, operate with a budget. Determine the absolute necessary expenses and create a budget to stay within that amount of money.

Once your business begins generating income, you can establish what your salary will be, and any other necessary expenses to add. Your budget should be adjusted every time your business income increases or decreases. Your budget should be based on revenue, not expenses. The goal is always for income to exceed expenses. The Elite Woman in

Business entrepreneur looks for ways to always contain and reduce expenses.

Unless you intend to operate a brick-and-mortar business, you most likely do not need to purchase or rent space to operate the business initially. Home offices and garage spaces are perfect beginner offices and work spaces.

I used my local UPS store for faxing, copying, etc. for most of the first year of my business, because the frequency of use did not justify buying the equipment. That decision saved me a ton of money. In my second year, I decided the bulk of that work could continue to be done the same way, and that is working out great for my business.

Here are more financial considerations for your start-up budget:

- *Cost of meeting with accountant and setting up your bookkeeping chart of accounts*
- *Cost of meeting with attorney*
- *Application fees for licenses, registrations, incorporations, etc.*
- *Writing articles of incorporation and corporation bylaws, if establishing a C-corporation or S-corporation*
- *Insurance policies*
- *Domain name registrations*
- *Website hosting plan, if a website is required*
- *Business checks*
- *Rent or lease payments for brick-and-mortar spaces*
- *All required equipment (notice the word "required")*
- *All required supplies (notice the word "required")*
- *Perhaps business cards — these are not the mainstay they used to be*
- *Quarterly income taxes*

Every business will have its own unique start-up expenses. Your accountant should be able to help you plan for your business. The Small Business Administration is also a great resource for start-up budgets. Depending on the type of business you are building, there may be a state or national association of similar businesses. With some research, you can gain insight into the typical start-up necessities. Have a plan, anticipate the amount it will cost, and allocate the money.

In the ELITE Business Building Foundations eCourse, I help you establish profit goals and to fund profit before any expenses. If you really want to build a profitable and sustainable business, be sure to check it out.

## Starting as a Side Hustle

If you decided this business will be a side business you will nurture and grow before making the leap into full-time entrepreneurship, there's one thing I want you to do: always pay yourself first! This can be a salary or distribution as a set percentage of business income.

It can become very easy to continue to generate income and not pay yourself. You can use the excuse I want to use that money to grow the business, to pay for x, y or z. Before you know it, you have been in business for years and personally never made a dime.

Remember my photography business, where I worked like crazy for FREE because I never paid myself? Well, I was working my tail off throughout ridiculous hours and generated five figures – almost six – but I never once took a distribution or paycheck. Why? I was investing in the business, buying equipment, working on branding, etc. Trust me, that became a real drag after a while.

## Investing in Yourself

The best advice I ever received as I started my consulting company came from Darren Hardy, my mentor at the time. He told me to allocate 10% of my earnings every year for personal development and education. I took that advice to heart and religiously do that every year. I can tell you that the return on my investment is always greater than the 10% I paid.

Commit to being a life-long learner. Regularly investing in your personal development and continued education needs to be considered early in your business. Investing in yourself with quality mentoring, education and coaching will always provide a return on your investment.

Start where you are and utilize resources you can afford and level-up your investment amount as your business becomes more successful. I started with free resources and now invest five figures a year in education and coaching.

## A Word of Caution

I want to end this part of the book about finances and legal aspects with a word of caution: You will invariably encounter someone, or many someone's, who tell you registering your business, obtaining licenses, getting insurance, having contracts, etc., is not necessary. They might even tell you they have owned a business for 20 years and never purchased insurance, registered as a legal business, hired an accountant, or had a professional do their taxes.

Basically, what they're telling you is that the local, state or federal government simply has not yet caught up to them! Eventually it will happen. The IRS audit, a claim or lawsuit over harms or damages or injury could happen at any moment.

Please disregard the naysayers that tell you to be less than a professional, legitimate, legal, and protected business. Yes, there are costs associated with doing it right the first time around, but in hindsight, the costs up-front for legality and protection are so much less than payments for failure to protect yourself.

I never want one of my readers or students or clients to be on the wrong end of the law or the IRS.

Most importantly, I want anyone associated with my brand to operate with the highest level of integrity.

And finally, I want you to be respected among other entrepreneurs. I promise you if you are skimping on these aspects, other entrepreneurs who are doing it right will lose all respect for you.

## Examples of What Not to Do

I believe in learning from mistakes, so here's my personal story about my photography business versus another local photographer — and what happened between us.

I was in business first and had been established in Arkansas for five years. Another photographer came onto the scene and basically copied my entire business model. She offered the same services at a fraction of the cost and quality, which is also when I noticed a significant drop-off rate of my lowest paying clients.

Did I panic? Not at all.

I expanded my marketing efforts to replace low paying clients with higher paying ones. I also wished her well. I watched her improve the quality of her work over the years. But, I could never respect the business she operated.

While the session fee for a portrait session with my business was $150 for up to a one-hour session, and the prints I ordered were from one of the most reputable printing labs in the U.S. (which required that every vendor be a legitimate business with all appropriate licenses), my "competitor" charged less than half of what I did and gave images to clients on CDs with delivery times months into the future.

Because I chose to operate my business in a way that was rooted in integrity, my competitor had to work multiple times over the same number of hours as I did in to earn the same amount of money. Because she gave the customer everything she produced in the portrait session, she had no hope of upselling or creating a sales opportunity with that client again.

I also knew I had nothing to worry about, because we had very different target markets: my ideal client wanted a luxury experience with high quality photographic art pieces; my competitor was aiming for clients who wanted the cheapest prices possible.

And, competing on price will never grow your business into the elite ones I coach my clients to create. The race to the lowest price is a race to the bottom and the first one there loses.

**There will always be competition. Choose to be different. Choose to be exceptional. Choose excellence. Choice to create value that supports what you charge.**

I also did everything I could to ensure I had all the correct licensure, paid all my taxes, was a member of the local Chamber of Commerce, and more. Unfortunately, my competitor did not do anything to ensure the longevity of her business in case of any mishaps and unfortunately, because of this, eventually went out of business due to something that could very well have been prevented if she had a simple insurance policy from the get-go.

Thanks to the ethical approach I had for my business, I was selected as Woman of the Year for my community. My business was voted Best of the Best eight out of ten years. I won the national Bride's Choice award six years in a row. I also had a steady stream of client testimonials that served my business well.

Even more importantly, I made friendships and formed relationships with my clients that will last a lifetime. I also gave back to the community, by helping to build one of the largest art shows in Arkansas in my community and supported charities that were close to my heart.

Again, my Core Values are Impact, Excellence and Service, which is not just something I put on my website — it's something I truly and deeply believe. My first mentor, Darren Hardy, had a tagline: Choose to be the Exception.

I chose to be the exception, even though the cost to operate was high, but the peace of mind and the payback (both monetarily, emotionally, and spiritually) is so much higher.

# Chapter 5 - Building Your Brand

*"A brand is the set of expectations, memories, stories and relationships that, taken together, account for a consumer's decision to choose your product or service over another." – Seth Godin*

Yes, you have a brand. Your brand is what other people say about your business when you are not around. It's how your business is perceived by the customer. A brand is not just a logo and the colors you choose.

Customers aren't looking for another cookie-cutter company who offers the same thing as everyone else. They are looking for an experience tailored to their needs, backed by genuine personal interaction. This is why branding is so important.

You do not need to hire an expensive branding company in the beginning. When your business is generating income, that can be an expense you budget for! At this stage, let's just work on crafting your brand story, and the look and feel of your brand.

**A brand is not just a logo - it is the total customer experience from first impression to long-lasting customer relationship.**

Branding is the process of forming memories, emotions and a relationship around your brand in the consumer's brain. The goal is to build such a strong connection and such strong belief that the consumer takes on your brand identity as their own. They use your brand to help define who they are as a person.

Is there any better example of branding than Harley Davidson? Talk about raving fans! Harley Davidson has created a culture around their brand, and the customers have taken on HD's brand identity as their own.

The first element of branding is knowing your customer. You accomplished that early in this book. This is who you tell your brand story to, and the person you want to brand to attract.

The second part is to identify what is unique about you, your company, and what you offer. You nailed that down earlier in the book, too. (Good job! Two really important key steps already done!)

Now, it's time to define your brand as a *person,* rather than as a logo or a written voice. If your company were a person, what type of person would that be? How would that person present themselves? How would they behave? How would they speak? How would this person gain the trust and support of the ideal customer?

**Brainstorm here:**

You are now ready to think about things like brand colors, tone of voice, serious or quirky, logos, etc.

When you're just getting started, make use of free or inexpensive tools available. Websites like upwork.com and fiverr.com have low-cost solutions for logo creation. Pinterest is a great source of inspiration for choosing your branding colors. Search brand mood boards to see examples companies have used to put their branding look together.

Branding is not a one-and-done exercise. Branding is about creating an experience, the desired experience for your customer. Branding happens with how your website or store is presented to your ideal customer. It happens when you have email or phone conversations with customers. It happens when you resolve customer complaints or issues. It happens as you create products and services, and how those are delivered to the customer.

Successful branding happens when a customer knows it is your business without looking at the name on the label, package, website, email, etc.

The experience and the identity is so strong and unique, it is immediately recognizable as your business, which is why the last thing you would ever want to do is to emulate your competitor's brand.

Let's work through some of the initial components:

*What colors do you feel express your brand? (It is totally okay to go off to Pinterest and have a look around the mood boards)*

*If you are artsy, do you have a concept for your logo? Sketch that here or write down the must-haves to communicate to your logo designer.*

*While you are at it, pick a font that you will always use in every piece of information or communication: (Later you can choose a second or third to add in, let's stay basic right now). You can do a web search for fonts to see examples and try out typing your business name to see how it will look.*

*How will you incorporate your brand colors into the brand?*

*Describe how you want to interact with customers:*

*Describe what you want the customer experience to feel like to the customer:*

*If you will deliver physical products, what does the brand packaging look like:*

*If you will own a storefront, what does it look like? What does it smell like? What is the arrangement or décor of the space?*

*What Is the personality of the brand? (Formal, Informal, quirky, authoritative, collaborative, comical, etc.)*

The personality will determine the voice of the brand. A business voice could be professional, friendly, service-oriented, promotional, conversational, informative, etc. But to be consistent, use this voice every time — in every email, phone call, consultation, sales meeting, customer interaction, on the website, in marketing materials, and on your social media profiles.

Truthfully, branding was a hard element for me. I struggled for the first year of my business. When I could afford a professional, I immediately put that into my budget. It was one of the best investments I have ever made. But, spending that money initially was not a priority, so I waited. You can, too.

Once you have all these details nailed down, look on websites like Upwork or fiverr.com to find someone who can take your ideas, colors, and logo and create a mood board for you. You should be able to get this very inexpensively. It will serve as a visual reference for the look and feel of your brand.

In combination with your core values, vision statement and mission statement – the brand will keep you centered on the mission critical elements of the brand. Your customers will love you for this!

**Getting Social**

Almost every business needs at least one social profile. Which one? That is always the first question. I have a better question for you. Where is your ideal customer most active?

You learned where your audience is hanging out in the market research phase. Wherever this is, this is where your business needs to be.

I'll be honest that my absolute favorite social channel is Twitter, probably because there are less photos of people's meals, less oversharing/TMI, and posts are short and to the point.

However, my ideal customer is NOT on Twitter. My ideal customer is on Facebook and increasingly on Instagram.

You did the research, and perhaps your ideal customer is on every available social media platform. But, where are they most active? Where do they spend the most social media time? Where do they comment or engage most? Where do they share most? That is where you must be.

I want to pass along some advice from Joe Pulizzi, who I met earlier this year. Joe is the CEO and Founder of Content Marketing Institute and bestselling author of the book, *Content, Inc.* He was kind enough to spend time with me after a keynote speech and gave advice I have fully taken to heart.

"Pick one main platform. Produce content on that platform consistently. Form relationships with the people who join / follow your social profile on that platform. Be persistent and produce content year after year. Offer value and make giving value one of your key objectives. Be authentic and share your expertise, knowledge, and wisdom."

Before that conversation, I was all over the place. Trying to be everything on every social media platform, even some I hated. This realization was such a relief to me! I almost immediately stopped everything except Facebook – because that is where my people are.

This is the perfect time to talk about what to do if you really dislike social media. Maybe that is not you, but I have plenty of friends who have zero social media accounts.

Here is what I must say about social media for business.

Use it as a complement to your other online presence, like a website, blog, membership site, or forum. Whatever your main online platform is, social media is just a boost, not a replacement.

Here are key points to remember:

Your friends / followers appear on your page or profile, but you do not own their information. Facebook, Instagram, twitter or whoever owns their personal information. You cannot consider social media followers to be a "list", as in your marketing list. At any given moment, the social platform could go away…remember Myspace? So, how you access or connect with your followers could disappear.

Online businesses are struggling now with the updated algorithm of Facebook, which will always be changing. You are not in control of what happens on social media. But you are in control of what happens on your own website or blog. Consider how you want to be your online presence in the form of a website or blog early, and do not think you can just exist on social media alone.

The second thing I will say about social media is do not fall into the numbers envy. *"So-and-so has tens of thousands of followers, I can never compete with that."* Sometimes the numbers are misleading. Often on Twitter and Instagram, those followers have been purchased. Sometimes they group has grown to a large number of followers, but hardly anyone is engaged on the page.

Remember, you are just starting out. Start where you are. Be authentic. Share value. Build relationships. In the long run, this is the winning formula. It will not happen overnight, but success never does.

This is also a great time to address what to do if you are terrified of the tech side of social media. Most likely you will need to set up a business profile on whatever platform you choose to focus.

Here are a couple of my go-to sources when I am feeling lost about where to start:

- YouTube is a great source for visual learners. If you want to watch someone do what needs to be done and then copy that, watching videos is a great way to learn. I host ELITE Women TV on YouTube and produce a weekly episode packed with tools and strategies to build, grow or scale your business.
- Google / Blogs. You can find unlimited information on anything you want to learn online. I typically start at Google and look for blog articles or online magazine articles that deal with the subject I am looking for.
- Your kids. Seriously, they know all the in's and out's of every social media platform on the planet. Chances are it will be a good bonding experience to learn something from them. I promise, they know how to do everything.
- For Facebook, specifically, they do have a forum that has articles and videos on how to do almost everything.

While it won't make you an expert, you can find resources to walk you through areas where you get stuck.

When it comes to your online presence, whether it is just a website or blog, or a full-out social media presence, look at your competitors. What information do they share? What types of posts do they share? How much engagement do they have on their posts, pictures and videos? You can learn a lot by researching their online presence. I am not suggesting you simply copy their format. Just dig in enough to gain some insight and inspiration.

The bottom line is not to be intimidated about setting up your social profiles. Use the tips above to get started. As revenue starts coming in, add contracting with a virtual assistant to spruce up your profile. For now, get started and create consistent content.

**Where are your people? Where is "your person"?**

Build your first business social media profile or page on that platform. Use your brand voice and identity to produce content and get engaged with your customers. Your following will not come overnight. But eventually you will attract your customers. Your vibe attracts your tribe.

I recommend buying the domain name for your business in the .club format. Re-direct that domain to your Facebook page. It's a great learning in consistent branding!

Now, I am not a social media marketing strategist, so I will not give you advice on marketing tactics, but I do know the advice Joe gave me is the real thing. People come on social media for entertainment, engagement and to be social. It's unlikely that they're specifically going on social media to be sold something, so be mindful of that.

In the entrepreneurial world, I highly suggest you employ the tactics of Gary Vaynerchuk in his book, *Jab, Jab, Jab, Right Hook*. Give, give, give, sell. Provide value and build relationships first and foremost. Only after you have given value time and again should you promote or ask for a sale.

Occasionally, business owners ask if they should you have more than one business social media profile. Maybe. Maybe not. That really will depend on your specific business, your ideal customer, and the industry standard. Perhaps a LinkedIn profile is all your business will need. That is all I have for my consulting business, because that is where the executives that hire me look for thought leaders and experts.

You can create social media profiles on as many platforms as you choose to reserve your business name. However, please do really think about Joe's advice – focus on one. When the following is large enough, branch out. In the early stages of your business, spreading yourself thin across multiple platforms is time consuming, over-whelming, and ineffective.

**Tapping into Expert Resources**

There are things your business needs that you are not prepared or equipped to provide. There are skills needed in your business that you do not possess. There are times when you doing something does not make logical or financial sense.

Be okay with that! Seriously, just be okay with it.

Being a solopreneur is fine. I am a solopreneur. I have zero employees in any of my three full-time businesses.

Initially, I figured out a way to do whatever needed to be done inside my business or for my business. Whether that meant learning the skill, finding the time, harnessing the energy, or just getting it done, I was the one at the helm.

Your business will operate much the same way in the beginning. But, at some point, you need to move beyond the sole worker bee and outsource both experts and talent.

I spent valuable time and energy learning skills I should not have tried to learn. The results? I never became the expert on what I tried to master, and still know very little. I spent countless hours trying to figure it out. It took me anywhere from twice to ten times the amount of time it would have taken an expert to get it done. It was frustrating and exhausting!

When I began my coaching business, I needed to up my online presence. From building a website, to developing sales funnels, creating landing pages, connecting each piece on the back-end. It. Was. Overwhelming. Wired the way I am, I set out to figure this all out on my own. I watched videos from the landing page service. I watched videos from the email service provider. I watched WordPress videos on website design. I started. I started over. I was driving myself insane.

Here's the thing, none of those things are my zone of genius. None of those things should be my number one priority. My number one priority is to create content, market and sell. Inside your business, you will have a zone of genius, whether you provide a product or a service. There are things that must be done that only you can or should do. It is true for every business.

When you are bootstrapping and trying to make every dollar you invest count in the beginning, think about time invested as well as money. If you are taken away from doing what brings in money, to work on something that does not immediately generate money, you are losing money. That was a hard lesson for me to learn. I like to take charge. I like to conquer. I like knowing I can figure things out. I finally did learn that I do not have to figure everything out. The things that I struggle with are someone else's zone of genius.

I wasted time and delayed generating revenue trying to get ramped up. I had to endure do-overs, because my original approach did not work. I went back to square one more than once when I did not get the results I needed.

I also ran myself ragged, working 16 – 20 hours a day, seven days a week, just trying to do everything myself. What is worse than having a 9-to-5 job that stresses you out, or that you hate? Owning a business that stresses you out and that you grow to hate!

You will need to learn what you can do for your business, what you should even attempt to do, and what you just should not do.

Here are ways to contract help:

- Bring someone on for a one-time project that can be purchased as a one-time stand-alone purchase.
- Bring someone on for a contract basis. They are not your employee. You are not required to pay taxes on the contract fee you pay them. You do not owe them any employee benefits. I use this method quite frequently.
- You can also outsource to virtual assistants through contract arrangements. Again, a virtual assistant (VA) is still not your employee. You determine the number of hours per week you want them to work and pay the contracted fee. They are the employee of the company you source them from. You can increase or decrease their hours at any time. Virtual assistants are great for routine, administrative tasks. Many are also especially talented, skilled and diverse. You can find a VA to do literally anything inside your business: maintain your website, manage social media, create sales funnels, handle customer relations, etc.

Use sites like www.fiverr.com and upwork.com, to find low-cost solutions to your needs in the beginning. Do not blow your start-up budget for the beginning with services you must go into debt to afford.

Back to my lead-in on this topic, when I began building my sales funnel, I invested in an email marketing service, a landing page creation service, and tried to figure everything out myself. Yet, I had all these questions: how do I get an opt-in to be added to my email marketing service? How do I connect that to my landing page? How do potential clients get directed to my shopping cart? Then, how will they get back to the Thank You page? And, how can they be added to my newsletter? Aargh!

I was literally ready to scream. I watched hours of how-to videos and read blogs, but I never figured it out completely. Time lost. Money lost.

Finally, I realized I could outsource this and was so happy knowing I did not have to watch another video or try one more day to figure it all out myself. Within a week, the contractor I hired had everything set up, connected, and running seamlessly. This was her zone of genius. What was hard for me, was easy for her because she was the expert.

Speaking of email providers, you might hear everyone in the online world telling you how vital it is to build an email list. This is a great way to stay in touch and build that essential know-like-trust factor with your ideal clients. Building your own list outside of social media is important if you plan to market online or generate any revenue online.

Put simply, this means that you advertise to get someone to provide you their email address, usually in exchange for something of value at no cost. They enter their email address and your email service provider collects the address and adds it to your email list. This book is too short to go into the value of having a list. Just note that building your own list becomes your asset. No one owns it or controls it but you, unlike social media followers.

For a free to low-cost email marketing service, try Mailchimp. This is a great starter service. As you build your list, you can upgrade once revenue is coming in. Remember as I said in the beginning to start where you are — you might see people in the industry using services like InfusionSoft, but know that the people you're looking up to likely have the resources to invest, and something like InfusionSoft is not only expensive, but also has many features you may not be able to initially use.

**Let me repeat: You do not have to become the expert in everything.**

I am incredibly happy working with women like you to build their business. I am not happy when I must set up the back-end operations of a sales funnel. And, knowing this, I now have the means to outsource what's not in my zone of genius.

You will encounter times like this, too, no matter what kind of business you are operating. It is totally okay to not be the expert at everything. Never be afraid to let go of control over things you should not be investing your time and energy into. Stay in your zone of genius!

I am a productivity and time management expert – having spent almost two decades working in process improvement. If you are interested in learning the success tips of highly successful entrepreneurs, please reach out to me and ask about the ELITE Productivity course.

**Just a Side Note**

Make the commitment to never stop learning and working on your personal development. I mentioned earlier that I invest 10% of my revenue into personal development and education every year.

I encourage you to do the same. I believe we are never finished learning, and should be lifelong learners. Successful entrepreneurs are committed to continuous learning.

I schedule personal development time every single day, first thing in the morning. That could take the form of listening to a podcast, reading a blog article, reading a chapter in a book, completing a module of an online course, or listening to a keynote speech. It primes my mind for success and focus for the remainder of the day.

You can commit whatever percentage you feel is appropriate to your personal development. You can also commit that percentage from your personal salary or your business revenue. I devote to 10% of my gross revenue of the business.

I also created an automatic savings transfer into a special savings account, solely for education, which is added monthly. This makes it seamless, so I am never tempted to skip saving for an investment I know will propel my business forward.

When I was just starting my businesses, I used mostly free resources. I saved money until I could afford to invest in a course or a conference / seminar. As I have built my business and paid off my personal debt, I can now afford to invest in more paid resources.

I still utilize a lot of free resources, like podcasts and blogs. In the beginning, The point is, I am always learning.

Be sure to also get an accountability partner. This is not someone you pay. This is someone who you regularly check in with, who can help you set goals, and who can hold you accountable for planned actions. You can have meetings with your accountability partner in-person meeting or over the phone. Know this is a two-way relationship, so be sure you provide the same value to each other. You can find an accountability partner within your industry, a networking organization, a course, a coaching program or similar program.

A great format to follow with an accountability partner is to set weekly goals. Your phone calls or video conferencing will be focused on whether you each achieved your goals for the previous week. What were the lessons? What did you struggle with? What were your wins for the week? When you spend time each week recording this information in preparation for the call, you can measure progress. Having an accountability partner, for me, has been huge in terms of my personal commitment and growth.

Ultimately, there is no substitute to working with a business coach. You may not be able to budget for the services of a private business coach in the beginning, yet almost every coach offers other programs, such as eCourses or group coaching programs, which are more affordable options during your start-up phase. This is an area I would **never** skimp on!

For the last two years, I have participated in group coaching, 1:1 coaching and a mastermind.

By participating in group coaching, I was able to access an expert in business development at a lower price point, and participate with other women at the same stage in my business. This opportunity helped me clarify my product suite and customer journey, as well as networking with other female entrepreneurs. If you are someone who benefits from a group environment and do not want the focus to be solely on you, group coaching is a great option. From what I learned in the group program, I was able to launch Elite Women in Business.

But at a certain point, I needed more specific education and support. Group coaching did not allow one on one focus on my business as much as I would have liked. Enter 1:1 coaching. It was a more of an investment, but every coaching session was dedicated to only me and my business goals. This definitely took me to the next level. It has been through one on one coaching that I am able to get individualized feedback and support. My business coach is a strategic partner inside my business. 1:1 Coaching helped me refine Elite Women in Business and develop my specific vision for the business, in a way I did not reach in group coaching.

A mastermind experience is a step beyond one on one coaching, and is for a group of people to come together and shared lessons learned, give support and advice, and is facilitated by a coach. I am in a mastermind group of twenty women who are all working on the same business strategy. Every meeting and call is focused on learning from each other and offering advice and support. We come together quarterly for networking and sharing. This experience has been so powerful I have already committed for another year.

In talking with people one of the most often objections I hear is "I cannot afford a coach." A very wise person once told me, "don't say I cannot afford it; figure out how you can afford it." I have found this to be so true with every investment level I have entered with my own coaching experiences. Every level up has been more of an investment, but I have committed to making my personal and business development a priority. Therefore, I can always figure out how to make the investment.

For example, in addition to the 10% of revenue I set aside for education, I ultimately decided the mastermind experience was so important I reduced the salary I take from my consulting business to cover the cost of the mastermind. Once your business is established, you will have options like this to tap into, as well.

Whether it is through one on one coaching, group coaching, mastermind experiences, conferences, seminars, or eCourses, the experience and knowledge you receive are like little assets you collect along the way. The networking opportunities and relationships built become invaluable over time. I have never failed to recoup my investments in coaching, and usually I gain back two to ten times what I invested.

In your start-up phase, take stock of your goals and identify the gaps in what you can do and where you need help launching. Give priority to investing in yourself in your budget. As you are building the foundation of your business, this is a critical time. Many mistakes can be made that are costly. Many frustrations can stack up that are stressful. Having some type of support from an expert hedges your bets, and provides valuable support that you are going to need. The minute you can afford working with a business success coach — do it!

## Going from Business Idea to Open for Business

I hope you finish this book and the pages are highlighted, written on, and folded over. I wrote it for that specific purpose. Through all my years as an entrepreneur I can honestly say I did not always do business the right way. But one thing I did do right is to try to learn from my mistakes.

One of the biggest mistakes I made for most of my entrepreneurial life was to just try to do everything alone, which has taught me two valuable lessons:

One, doing it the hard way does not make you a hero. It makes you stubborn. Staying in my zone of genius makes me a happier and more productive, and profitable entrepreneur.

Two, building a business on a solid foundation with an intentional plan, not only for the business, but also for my life was one of the best decisions I have ever made. Looking back and comparing my photography business with my current businesses, there is no comparison.

I really had no life before. No time for family. No time for friends. No time for fun. No time to take care of myself. Stress, anxiety, debt, non-stop work – you could barely call it a life.

When I became a full-time entrepreneur, I spent time asking myself questions about the kind of life I wanted to live. I went about creating a business that fit into that plan after I knew the answers.

My life today looks very different. I regularly take time off, and at least one day every week is a completely unplugged day, where I fully disconnect from all things business and do whatever I want.

I have been blessed that I was able to take my whole family on several adventures this year. We cruised the Caribbean over Christmas and New Year's, saw a throw-back 90's pop group in Vegas this spring, and just visited Alaska and British Columbia. I don't say that to brag. I tell you this to highlight the importance of making time for what you love. For me, that is my family and travel. The memories and experiences we have shared the last two years – I cannot even begin to put a price tag on it. Like the commercial says… Priceless!

My lifestyle today allows time for creative projects, rest, exercise, family, friends, travel – all the things that are important to me. I have a plan for my life and my business. I plan for taxes and annual business expenses. I plan for business emergencies. I plan for profit. And, I plan for me.

All of this is possible because I focused first on building a solid business foundation. I then concentrated on eliminating my personal debt. And finally, I designed my business to fit into that kind of lifestyle.

Is every day smooth sailing? Of course not. But, just like the nursery rhyme, my business can withstand a few setbacks and "storms" because the foundation is solid.

I hope you have used this book as your personal workbook to get your business open. We have literally walked through every step of the process to open your business together aside from product creation, which is beyond the scope of this book. The exact steps I followed to launch my six-figure business.

The length of time it takes to launch your business will be different for everyone. I opened my consulting business within 30 days, while my coaching business took multiple months. Life, drive, dedication, learning, and opportunity all play a factor.

You may choose to leave the 9-to-5 behind and go all-in with opening a business. Or, you may choose to start a business on the side. Either way, you have a roadmap to launch your business into the world with this book.

I cannot wait to hear your success story!

Please email me WHEN your business is open and successful, I want to feature success stories on my blog and social media, so be sure you let me know. I would also love to hear your feedback, struggles, and questions.

I'm beyond grateful any time I know I have helped another woman over 40 leave a burned-out career and create a profitable business. When I hear her say she is living a life she now loves, I'm over the moon.

So, please share your story with me.

Wishing you all the success in the world,

*Cheryl*

# ABOUT THE AUTHOR

Cheryl Mauldin is a business strategy coach, Founder of Elite Women in Business, CEO of Relentless Consulting, Inc., author and keynote speaker. She provides premium coaching services to women over 40 who are ready to leave their burned out 9 to 5 and create the business and life of their dreams. She has been featured in Success Magazine as a Thoughtleader ®, on the EOFire podcast and many other blogs and podcasts for entrepreneurs.

She lives in Arkansas, loves to travel, read, and photography. She is mom to three beautiful daughters, Brittany, Lindsay and Hannah.

*Connect with Cheryl*

Blog: http://cherylmauldin.com

Facebook: http://elitewomeninbusiness.club

Elite Women in Business Podcast

YouTube: http://elitewomen.tv

Twitter: http://www.twitter.com/cherylmauldin

Email: cheryl@cherylmauldin.com

Access to the free mini-course: http://elitewomeninbusiness.com

## Special Offer

### Give me 12 weeks and I will show you how to build the business of your dreams!

Stop slugging it out day after day at an uninspiring, mentally draining job, and create the business of your dreams.

Be able to do the thing you were born to do – fulfill the purpose you were put on earth to do.

Launch your business on a solid foundation that is set up from day one to be profitable and help you achieve the lifestyle you want.

In my 12-week eCourse, ELITE Business Building Foundations (https://elite-courses.thinkific.com/courses/elite-foundations) you will get the tools and resources to make smart decisions in your business launch phase to set you up for success.

There is no fluff, no BS, no magic bullets, or unicorns. Just solid strategies and practical advice that I used to create multiple six-figure revenue in the business of my dreams.

**My business has made the WORLD of difference to me, my family and the lives of the clients I work with.**

Imagine how different your life would be if you could get up every morning and do work that inspires you, makes you feel alive, and was fun.

Imagine how different your life could be if you were pursuing and building your dream, instead of someone else's dream.

Imagine how different your life could be if you were in charge of how much money you generate, instead of depending on someone else to value your worth with an hourly wage or annual salary.

With over thirty years entrepreneurial experience, I know a thing of two about what works and what does not. I made my share of mistakes along the way and went through the business school of hard knocks.

Along the way, I have worked with some of the smartest minds in the entrepreneurial world, such as Darren Hardy and Stacy Tuschl. I have also invested tens of thousands of dollars in education, mentoring and coaching. I have been featured in Success Magazine, the EOFire podcast, and others for my business success and strategies.

Now I coach women over 40 who are trapped in the 9-to-5 game of trading time for dollars at a job they have grown to hate, but feel stuck. I help women just like you create their own brilliant lives and businesses. I run private coaching programs, group coaching programs, and host private retreats.

But, to you, none of that will mean anything until you take the first step. Until you are ready to invest in your own success and take action, not much is going to change for you.

*It's okay if at this point you are scared, overwhelmed, and confused.*

*It's okay if you have no idea where to start.*

*It's okay if you feel like you have waited too late in life.*

I was exactly where you are before I left Corporate America and created the business of my dreams. I was almost 50 years old, in debt, with little retirement saved, and felt trapped.

But I believed there was a better way and a better life. I knew I was meant to do more with my life. Had I not taken action and invested in myself, I would still be punching that time clock every Monday morning, working on someone else's dream.

### It's time for you to make a decision.

Do you want more of the same old thing for the rest of your life? Going to work day in and day out facing the same frustrations, bumping your head against the glass ceiling, wondering how you will ever make it to retirement.

Or, are you ready to claim your greater purpose? Step up and create the life you know deep inside you were meant to live. Create a solid and profitable business doing what you love and what you are good at.

Trust me, your life will never be the same, and you will never look back and say "what if."

If you are ready to take the first step in creating your dream life, say YES to your life, say YES to creating your brilliant business, you are ready for ELITE Business Building Foundations. (https://elite-courses.thinkific.com/courses/elite-foundations)

**Learn more**

## So, what's in the course?

The exact blueprint I used to leave my 9-to-5 and launch a business

- Specific strategies for refining your business idea and doing market research
- How to niche down to your ideal customer
- Discovering your unique selling proposition
- Identifying strengths, weaknesses and opportunities
- Business structure
- How to build your business model and sales funnel
- Business finances and budget
- Making profit a priority
- Charging what you are worth
- Setting 100 day goals
- Designing your ideal life
- Money mindset
- Investing in your success

**The full course is jam-packed with information, value, and BONUSES!** We all love bonuses, right?

**In this course, you'll receive:**

- 12 Modules

- LIVE Q&A call

- Access to private Facebook Group

- Bonuses! And extra training

- Discounts to Future Live Events

Each lesson in the course comes with a value-packed workbook to help you get the most value from each lesson.

**BONUS:** There will be a free Q&A call mid-way through the course and at the end where you can pick me brain. These live calls are the perfect time to ask questions, validate your ideas, and go even deeper with your learning.

**BONUS:** As you finish this course, and wonder, what next? I'm giving you access to my own 8-week Launch Plan as a special bonus!

Plus, other exciting bonus content!

This course regularly sells for $1497.

**Yours today, for only $997 – for a limited time!**

I know how intimidating it can be to launch your own endeavor, especially if you're a successful woman after the age of 40.

That's what kept me in a job I no longer loved for a decade too long.

It is also scary to jump in as an entrepreneur especially after you have built a comfortable life. Yet, that dream keeps playing over and over in your head.

I know, because it was the same for me.

I do not want you to hold yourself back any longer. Let's launch your brilliant business idea out into the world, and start creating a life you love. Once where you are excited to jump out of bed every day because you love what you do!

I designed this course for you! Let's do this!

**Enroll today and save $500. This is a LIMITED time offer.**

From business idea to launch in 12-weeks!

## Learn more

(https://elite-courses.thinkific.com/courses/elite-foundations)